The Revolt of the Young

Modern Intellectual and Political History of the Middle East
Mehrzad Boroujerdi, *Series Editor*

Other titles in Modern Intellectual and Political History of the Middle East

Becoming Turkish: Nationalist Reforms and Cultural Negotiations in Early Republican Turkey (1923–1945)
Hale Yılmaz

The Essentials of Ibāḍī Islam
Valerie J. Hoffman

Ethnicity, Identity, and the Development of Nationalism in Iran
David N. Yaghoubian

The International Politics of the Persian Gulf
Mehran Kamrava, ed.

Jurji Zaidan and the Foundations of Arab Nationalism
A Study by Thomas Philipp

Mirror for the Muslim Prince: Islam and the Theory of Statecraft
Mehrzad Boroujerdi, ed.

Pax Syriana: Elite Politics in Postwar Lebanon
Rola el-Husseini

Raging Against the Machine: Political Opposition under Authoritarianism in Egypt
Holger Albrecht

The Revolt of the Young

Essays by Tawfīq al-Hakim

Translated by Mona Radwan

Foreword by Roger Allen

Syracuse University Press

Syracuse, New York 13244-5290

First Edition 2015
15 16 17 18 19 20 6 5 4 3 2 1

Introduction originally appeared in *Al Rowad: The Eminent Scholars Series (Book 4) Essays in Language and Literature, In Honour of M.M.Enani.* Editor: Loubna Youssef and Co-Editor Maher Farid. Editorial Board: Mohamed Elkhosht and Amani Badawy. Cairo: Cairo Univ. Center for Language and Translation Press, 2012.

Essays translated from *Thawrat Elshabaab* (Cairo: Adaab Publisher, 1984).

∞ The paper used in this publication meets the minimum requirements of the American National Standard for Information Sciences—Permanence of Paper for Printed Library Materials, ANSI Z39.48-1992.

For a listing of books published and distributed by Syracuse University Press, visit www.SyracuseUniversityPress.syr.edu.

ISBN: 978-0-8156-3368-6 (cloth) 978-0-8156-5300-4 (e-book)

Library of Congress Control Number: 2014953848

Manufactured in the United States of America

To the memory of my dear mother

Mrs. Afaf Khalifa

Tawfīq al-Hakim was born in Alexandria in 1898 and studied law in Paris before becoming the Arab world's leading dramatist as well as a major short-story writer and man of letters. He is the author of seventy plays, a number of novels and short stories, and an autobiography.

Mona Radwan, an assistant professor in the Department of English at Cairo University, specializes in the twentieth-century novel. She has also taught at three private Universities in Cairo. Dr. Radwan wrote weekly in the well-known Egyptian newspaper *Aldostor* from 2011 to 2012. She has given a number of lectures on Egyptian writers at Pittsburgh University. She has also participated in various international conferences such as the ACLA and WOCMES conventions. Her PhD on *Aspects of War Neuroses in Pat Barker's Regeneration Trilogy* was published in 2012. She is currently a member of the translation committee at the Supreme Council for Culture in Egypt.

Contents

Foreword

ROGER ALLEN

Tawfīq al-Hakim (1898?–1987) has long been acknowledged as one of the most important figures in the history of modern Arabic literature. His most significant role was in the realm of theater, where he served as a pioneer figure in turning what had been a popular and highly participatory genre of public performance into something with more literary pretensions. He wrote a large number of plays that echoed the predominant themes of the times in which he struggled to find the dramatic techniques and language levels to suit the Egyptian (and larger Arabic-speaking world's) cultural and social heritage and their expectations for a new kind of twentieth-century literature. He was also a major contributor to the development of Arabic fiction, predominantly through a series of novels but also in short-story form. In all these genres, he endeavored not only to develop his craft but also to reflect on the pressing issues of the day.

Thus the play *Ahl al-kahf* (*People of the Cave*, 1933) and the novel *'Awdat al-rūh* (*Return of the Spirit*, 1933) were concerned with the idea of rebirth, and specifically of a new sense of Egyptian identity boosted by both a fervent nationalist movement and an increased awareness of the greatness of Egypt's past fostered by the discovery of the treasures of Tutankhamun's tomb in 1922. While the novel *`Usfūr min al-sharq* (*Bird from the East*, 1937) reflects his ideas about the relative value of different cultural norms and the problems of modernization in Egypt, his wonderful portrayal of rural Egypt, *Yawmiyyāt nā'ib fī al-aryāf* (*Diary of a Country Prosecutor*, 1937, or, in English translation, *The Maze of Justice*, 1947), is a direct product of his own legal experiences following his return to his homeland after a prolonged stay in France, as his alter-ego character, the prosecutor, confronts the need to apply French law to uncomprehending Egyptians in the provinces. In the 1940s, he was able to hone his dramatic skills by responding to a newspaper's request that he compose a series of one-act plays; the resulting works focused on particular social and political issues and in the process provided highly accurate portraits of various Egyptian character types. A fine example is *Ughniyat al-mawt* (*Death Song*, 1950), a short play portraying the family tensions that arise as a consequence of the tradition of revenge killings in Upper Egypt.

It turns out that among the many members of the younger generation of Egyptians who were influenced by the works of al-Hakim was an army officer who in 1954 was to become President Gamal `Abd al-Nāsir (Nasser). The famous playwright welcomed the 1952 Egyptian revolution almost immediately with a play entitled *Al-Aydī al-nā'imah* (*Soft Hands*, 1954), in which a former prince of the royal family acknowledges the profound changes that have taken place and volunteers to participate in the work of creating a new kind of society. By the end of the same decade, however, al-Hakim, like many other intellectuals, was beginning to see the negative side of the new society that had emerged. His famous play *Al-Sultān al-hā'ir* (*The Sultan's Dilemma*, 1960), which was a great success on stage, is set in the Mamlūk past of Egypt but is at the same time a scarcely concealed question mark about the legitimacy of authority and the ways in which it can be abused.

Following Nasser's death in 1970, al-Hakim published (significantly in Beirut, not in Cairo) *`Awdat al-wa`y* (*Return of Consciousness*, 1974) in which his misgivings about Nasser's presidency and the course of the Egyptian revolution were spelled out; given the president's known admiration for al-Hakim as a writer and intellectual, the playwright asked himself why he had not spoken out sooner. However, the presidency of Nasser's successor, Anwar al-Sādāt, was to prove at least as unsympathetic to the role of writers and intellectuals in Egypt, if not more so. A "Writers Union" was formed in 1975, and writers were required to join and sign off on a morality code. Najīb Mahfūz, Tawfīq al-Hakim, Yūsuf Idrīs, and Lewis `Awad—a veritable "who's who" of Egyptian literature at the time—refused to join and were banned from publishing for a short time, until saner heads determined that the entire situation was ridiculous.

I have discussed al-Hakim's career in this way (and with a reckless brevity and selectivity) in order to show that he was not only a major literary figure for some sixty years of the twentieth century—an era of enormous change in Egypt and the Arabic-speaking world—but also a public intellectual, addressing himself to the pressing issues of the day in a wide variety of genres. With all that in mind, it should not surprise us to learn that among what one might term his "nonliterary" works is the text translated here, *The Revolt of the Young* (1984), with its uncanny harbingers of issues raised by the events that have occurred in Egypt over twenty years since his death in 1987. Like most revolutionary movements, the uprisings of 2011, and specifically those that occurred in Egypt following the initial movement in Tunisia, brought together a widely disparate group of people with very different backgrounds and aspirations—secularists and Islamists, city-dwellers and farmers from the countryside, young and old, all of them focused on the urgent need to rid themselves of a dictatorial and corrupt regime—in Egypt's case, that being a disarming echo of the motivations behind the earlier revolution of 1952. However, subsequent events have shown that, while the quest for liberation *from* something (and the Arabic word for liberation, "Tahrīr," gives its name to Cairo's central square) usually manages to bring various political and social groups together in a unified movement advocating change, the subsequent process of liberation—freedom *to do* something and *to become* something different—proves considerably more complex and often confrontational. That situation describes, sadly, the Egypt of December 2012 as I write these words. It is in such a context that al-Hakim's *The Revolt of the Young* presents to its readers a voice from the past, one that seeks to offer comment and counsel to present generations of Egyptians in all their variety.

In fact, that very term, "generations," is an obvious point of concern for al-Hakim in this work, in that it makes its way into a number of chapter titles. He starts, however, as I have done in the previous paragraph, with some thoughts about the revolutionary process itself. In the chapters that follow, he focuses on the young and their role in the continuing development of Egyptian society, one that over the course of the last century and a half has witnessed foreign occupation, an experiment in parliamentary democracy within a monarchical system, a socialist revolution characterized by both successes and failures, the emergence of a dictatorial presidency, and now what might be regarded—in view of these previous political and social models—as the predictable emergence of a complex political scenario currently dominated by groups with varyingly strong ties to the tenets of Islam. It is a stunning ride through history, and the future remains very much to be determined. Al-Hakim himself did not live long enough to witness the most recent phases of this elongated and often disruptive process of experiment and change, but in this text he focuses on the institution that he regards as crucial to any forward progress, namely the family and its generations. In so doing, he provides us with an insight into both his own immense erudition—references to both Arab and other cultural traditions—and his personal devotion to Egypt, a feeling that, if anything, is amplified by his experiences abroad and especially in France (and we recall that, as part of his public persona in Egypt, the beret was an essential element of his clothing).

The succession of chapters swings easily between past and present time, as al-Hakim recalls conversations and incidents from his life and then focuses on their relevance to the present day and the concerns of its youth. When we bear in mind his status as a dominant icon of modern Arabic literature, it is no surprise to find him offering advice to younger writers (even venturing into the realms of modern poetry). His summary is particularly telling:

> Our literature in the next twenty or thirty years may make our generation eligible for the task of guidance and formation, but it will hand the actual leadership and direct models to the young writers. With these examples before them, they will give the literary scene a new color.
>
> This is their responsibility . . . What a great responsibility!

After some chapters that advocate the need for a greater sense of morality (with al-Hakim indulging in a duly learned tilt toward Faust), we come to the final, provocatively titled chapter, "The Case of the Twenty-First Century." It does not take the form of specific advice or comment about the author's homeland, but is rather a detailed account of a visit to the United States in the company of an American reporter and a lengthy "transcript" of a trial in which four young Americans are accused of plotting to blow up the Statue of Liberty (hence presumably the use of "case" in the original Arabic title). The cross-examination provides for a discussion of the nature and bases of American political activity, both local and international, and the young defendants say a great deal about their view of the role that the young need to play in order to transform the values of the society and to correct what they perceive as the errors of the past (in this particular case, the Vietnam War):

> [Attorney:] "Do you think that young people of the world are united in this direction?"
>
> [Defendant:] "On the contrary. Each nation has its own unique conditions, and what applies to one society doesn't exactly apply to another. Young people themselves differ from one another. But my words are directed to a society like our technological and capitalist society."
>
> "Do young people around the world unite in certain things in spite of the differences in their societies, peoples, and races?"
>
> "Yes! It is the way they sense the spirit of the new age. It is the way young people all over the world feel regarding the unity of the age, the world, and the future that is liberated from what is antiquated and worn out."

The relevance of all this to the present day and the question of values in the United States is further underlined when the prosecution raises another issue in court: both defendants have requested to be married to partners of the same sex, that being, needless to say, a political football in the United States of 2012–13 but also certainly a radical gesture when al-Hakim was still alive. As the trial comes to a close, one of the defendants is asked the question that seems to be hovering over not only this particular court case in New York but also the function of revolutions in no matter which venue:

> [Attorney:] "What do you mean here by the revolution?"
>
> [Defendant:] "I mean the real revolution of young people, which began like all revolutions with some aspects and the refusal of guardianship over their new lifestyle. They want to feel that something has changed in their lives and to begin bearing their huge responsibilities to change the face of the world."
>
> "And how can they change the face of the world? By disfiguring its features?"
>
> "Yes, its bad and ugly features. You must remember that these new generations whom you see outwardly having fun, are after all those who fill the seats in universities and libraries, wholeheartedly engaged in carrying out research in labs using the microscope. They will be the ones to make an inventory of and analyze all the great and useful achievements of humanity, to add to them and transfer them to the twenty-first century."

Thus wrote Tawfīq al-Hakim all those years ago.

Acknowledgments

I would like to thank Professor Galila Ann Ragheb for revising the book. Her efforts are warmly appreciated. Professor Ragheb's moral support throughout the years is greatly esteemed. She is somebody I truly cherish and deeply respect.

I would also like to extend my thanks to Professor Roger Allen for his patience and his support. His superb foreword adds to the value of this work.

Thanks are due to Professor Moustafa Riad, Professor Hussein Hammouda, and my colleagues Dr. Omia Khalifa, Dr. Rania Gouda, and Dr. Khaklid Tawfiq, whom I have consulted on a number of issues concerning my translation. I am grateful to them for their guidance.

I wish to thank the whole Syracuse team who were very helpful and worked arduously on this book. I am greatly indebted to them.

Translator's Introduction

I found the Arabic copy of *The Revolt of the Young: The Case of the Twenty-First Century* (1984, *Thawrat Elshabaab*) among books belonging to my late mother, and the title intrigued me. Having read it, I immediately decided to translate it as I thought it deserved to be available in English for those who are interested in Arabic literature. By the time the January 25 Revolution (2011) took place in Egypt, I had already finished translating the book but was even keener on editing it and looking for a publisher.

It turned out to be a fascinating collection of essays for a number of reasons. First and foremost, it sheds so much light on this great pioneer figure in Arabic literature. Al-Hakim was both a prolific and an influential writer as well as a great thinker. He wrote over seventy plays, eleven novels, and twenty-five collections of essays. Interestingly, he also wrote verse both in Arabic and French. He experimented in new genres such as a "dramatized novel" entitled *Bank of Worry* (1967) and "philosophical dialogues" as in *Dialogue with a Planet* (1974). A number of essays are concerned with the future, such as *A Journey to the Future* (1957), which he classifies as a "prophetic play." In 1980, he wrote a collection under the title of *Challenges of the Year 2000*.

This interest in the future is undoubtedly apparent in *The Revolt of the Young*. The clash between generations and the revolt of youth that loom large in *The Revolt of the Young* have been two of my main concerns as a rebellious woman growing up in Cairo. Al-Hakim wonders in chapter 13, "Is the gap between generations an inevitable one that cannot be altered? Or is it possible to correct this situation through understanding and cooperation?" He offers his solution in the same chapter and throughout this collection of essays. It also reveals the tense relationship between the writer and his son and how al-Hakim was able to resolve this tension before his son's untimely death. I believe that this book deserves to be in the limelight as it predicts the revolt of Egyptian and American young people socially and culturally if not politically in the twenty-first century. In chapter 19 he predicts that the resurrection will happen at the hands of young people just like in the Egyptian myth of Osiris and Horus. Some young Egyptian rebels from the April 6 movement, interviewed on Egyptian television in 2011, stated that they were inspired by al-Hakim's book *The Revolt of the Young*. One of them had the book with him in this interview and referred to it a number of times.

One of the challenges in translating this book was Tawfiq al-Hakim's style. It has been described by some critics as elevated and abstruse classical Arabic. The syntax is intricate. Al-Hakim's punctuation is unusual as he used hundreds of exclamation marks that I had to remove so that the English text would be acceptable. He used a great many ellipses (. . .) to show that he was contemplating an issue or instead of using a comma. I replaced most with either a period or a comma. One of the most difficult words I had to grapple with is in al-Hakim's introduction, where he was trying to differentiate between "revolution" and "upheaval"; the words in Arabic are "althawra" (الثوره) and "alhoga" (الهوجه). I checked the latter word in various dictionaries and asked most of the translators I know and the majority told me that "upheaval" would be the best equivalent in English. I agree it is but I am still not fully satisfied. The other words I thought of were "public disorder," "commotion," and "turmoil." I believe it is all the above.

Another stimulating element in this collection is al-Hakim's erudite style. There are myriads of cultural allusions to Western, Asian, and Arab works and writers. I decided to use footnotes to help the casual readers know who these writers are. He hardly ever mentioned the full citations he made use of in writing this book, and he did not include a bibliography or works cited. In his citations he usually refers to the author or/and title of the book but almost never the page number, publisher, or the date. I decided to keep the citations the way he wrote them, although I added the year of publication of the books he mentions to make it more reader friendly.

According to al-Hakim, young people have been the sparks of most revolutions around the world. One of the young people in the story (chapter 20) explains why the young carry out revolutions: "Because they are the ones who will see the twenty-first century. They want to pass on to it a better society. That is the issue. We young people cannot permit this corrupt society to cross the threshold of the new century. We will do everything in our power to pave the way for the new century with new ideas, just as the French Revolution of the nineteenth century paved the way for new ideas. . . ." In modern Egypt, the 1952 Revolution was led by young army officers. In the twenty-first century, in Tunisia, Egypt, Syria, and many other Arab countries, young people played a major role in the so-called Arab Spring. They revolted against the totalitarian regimes of the older generations. Since 2010 until this day, young people are still struggling socially and politically to achieve, as the popular slogan chanted all over Egypt says, "bread, freedom, and social justice." It is an ongoing revolution. It struck again in Egypt on June 30, 2013, against the Muslim Brotherhood regime, which did not fulfill the dreams of the young or old revolutionaries of 2011. The "Tamaroud Movement" led by young Egyptians together with the rest of the nation toppled the government and President Mohamed Morsy with the help of the army.

But why did the young Egyptian rebels fail to rule in 2011? Al-Hakim offers an answer—though he was referring to young people's revolt against De Gaulle's regime: "young people have not formed their own strongholds yet, being new to their revolution and their own sense of self. They do not yet have clear organized ideas. It is like the onset of any revolution when the old strongholds are destroyed and it stands at a loss for some time not knowing what to do next. . . . The more they rebel, the more the previous generation entrench themselves in their strongholds and the dividing gap between the generations become wider." Hence the old strongholds are still ruling in Egypt.

This rebellious spirit in the young does not manifest itself solely in the Middle East, but it is inherent in many angry young men and women in the West too. During the last century in the United States, for instance, university students protested against Vietnam, which al-Hakim refers to in the last chapter of this book. This century witnessed various demonstrations and sit-ins called "Occupy Wall Street." In France, there were fierce riots against housing problems, unemployment, poverty, police brutality, and racial discrimination in 2005. Protesters burnt cars, destroyed public property, and caused chaos in Paris and many other towns in France. Yet none of the above protests could be dubbed revolutions.

Al-Hakim's analytic and at times visionary outlook into the past, present, and future is beyond a shadow of a doubt valuable. His book inspires.

Mona Radwan
Cairo University

The Revolt of the Young

Introduction

Every revolution is a sign of vigor and youth is the most vigorous stage in life, so it is no wonder that revolutions are led by young people. One can scarcely find a revolution that has been led by the elderly because old age involves the diminution of vigor.

If a revolution is connected with vigor, so it should be a stimulant for such vigor and should refresh it. Otherwise, such a revolution would be deemed an "upheaval."

The distinction between "revolution" and "upheaval" is that the latter sweeps up with it both the good and bad, just as the turbulent wind does with both green leaves and withered ones, the fruitful tree and the barren one. A "revolution," however, retains what is useful and derives strength thereof. It does away with what is useless, worn out, that which impedes vigor, shuts out fresh air, and stands in the way of renewal and development.

However, the process is not always so simple. For "revolution" and "upheaval" sometimes, if not always, intermingle. To prove and establish itself, a revolution resorts to the violence of "upheaval" in order to uproot everything that came before it and thus takes credit for every new blessing and renders the history of everything its own. This state of things does not change unless the revolution feels strong enough and realizes that it has a special identity, a distinctive character and a solid base in public history. At that point, it scorns and discards the element of "upheaval" to return confidently to the public history of the nation and place all values in their rightful position. It would also downsize itself and forge a place within the natural evolution of a rising nation. If we grasp this, it becomes easier to understand the movements of the new generations or what is nowadays called "the revolt of the young."

When we were young, we all experienced a strong desire to overcome certain restrictions. This is an aspect of vitality, movement, liberation, and self-assertion. In order to assert our identity and establish our individuality, it became inevitable to separate ourselves from our predecessors. Our means of separation were that taken by every revolution at its outset, namely, the rejection of everything the predecessors said. In our youth, the gulf between parents and children was not as wide as it is now. At that time, the world had not yet witnessed world wars or ingenious inventions. Everything was set in fixed molds and kept in sealed boxes; the external world was secure, slumbering beneath its observed customs and sacred traditions.

Now, however, we are in a dynamic age surging with continuous changes, with intellectual, scientific, and political movements that transcend anyone's imagination. Nothing is stagnant, nor is it allowed to be; nothing is regarded as sacred. On the contrary, everything is subject to research and discussion.

The means of communication among nations, such as the radio, television, and satellite, have helped to spread all sorts of ideas, whether liberal, unruly, refined, or base. In such a world as the one we live in today, what is the effect of the media on young people who want to assert their identity and have a say in the formation of their character and a role in building the future?

We should be aware of all these facts and take them into consideration in dealing with young people today. It is our duty to make them realize that if they have the right to revolt, they must distinguish between "revolution" and "upheaval." They have to be able to distinguish between what is worth keeping and adding to, and what should be cast away from the path of development and the new age.

We should be wary of preaching to or advising young people on every occasion, ignoring what is essential by constantly referring to their appearance, thinking it is the end of the world if young people adopt certain fashions of dress or hairstyles. We forget that in our youth at the beginning of the twentieth century, young men who wore turbans chose bright colors for their traditional "*jubbah*"[1] and "*kaftan*,"[2] such as lemon yellow, purple, and pistachio green. As for young men who wore fezzes,[3] they used to follow the latest fashion in trousers from the tight-fitting, the wide Charleston, to the tapered. Sometimes they sported whiskers or pointed moustaches, and then there was the clean-shaven look, which was regarded as effeminate at that time. Today, being clean-shaven is widespread among young and old. All these are matters of no account now. Whenever adults make an issue of them, they are considered trivial-minded by young people and immediately lose their confidence and respect.

We are, at present, in an age characterized by mobility of thought, and we cannot deal with the revolt of the young unless we look at it within the framework of reflection and the essence of its nature.

1. *Jubbah* is a long, loose outer garment with wide sleeves worn by both sexes in the Arab world and India.

2. *Kaftan* is a long coat-like garment made of rich fabric and worn in the East.

3. Fezzes are men's felt caps in the shape of a flat-topped cone, usually red with a black tassel from the crown, worn chiefly in the eastern Mediterranean region.

Let us give youth the freedom to choose the inner and outer form of their lives as imposed by their new age. We should ask of them only one thing: to have a comprehensive and profound understanding of the civilization that formed and nurtured them, so that they would protect, develop, and add to the best of it and cast out, change, or wipe out whatever is evil and false. For the future of this civilization is in young people's hands alone; its image tomorrow will be as they imagine and form it. So let there be a revolt of the young.

But they should always remember the difference between "upheaval" and "revolution."

Tawfīq al-Hakim

1

The Link between the Generations

"Generations are linked together in nations as the vertebrae are linked in the body."

Life is made up of links in a chain, and every generation should link hands with the following one. If this happened in a nation, it would be well formed and sound, like the healthy body with its linked vertebral column; if not, it would be unhealthy and unsound, the links of its existence separated; its backbone would crumble and the nation could no longer exist. Since it is the leaders' task to look ahead to the next five to ten years to plan for the future, it is also their task to prepare the men who will be the future leaders; thus the wheel of progress would not cease to turn.

Intellectual output, like any other production, should not deviate from this principle. Intellectuals, before all others, should look ahead to the intellectual life of the years to come and make preparations for others to take their place, paving the way for new talents to appear and ripen. The question ever in mind is, what will happen in the next ten or twenty years? Can hopes be pinned on a group of men of letters whose role will be to take their turn in the front ranks and hold up the torch of literature and intellectual thought in this country? Or is it, as the saying goes, that "Things cannot be better than they are!"

In my opinion, the possibility of creativity is ever present; it is alive and moving in time and place. It is not linked only to the past but is like a tree that extends its branches and grows with the changing of the seasons: the colors of its leaves change, it blossoms and bears fruit, its past is linked to its present and its present is linked to its future. One effort is built upon another, talents are the product of other talents, creativity leads to more creativity, one fruit produces another, and all rotate in an orbit that will never cease till the end of time.

Today, if we walked in the garden of modern Arabic literature, we will find trees filled with the sap of life and diverse flowers of art, needing only that we look at them with pleasure and imagine how tall they will grow in the future, for nothing could spoil or lay waste to this garden more than to always see its trees as small bushes that will never grow large or cast pleasant shade. We should be trained to see things and persons in perspective. We should accustom ourselves to see things as they will be in the future, not only in the present, and know how to read the future through the lines of the present. If we are capable of doing that, we would no doubt find new pens in the various literary fields that will come to the fore in the next ten or twenty years, exactly as was the case of the leading figures in literature of the past ten or twenty years.

The garden of youth is filled with countless beautifully scented flowers. All that we aim for here is to consolidate hopes for our literary future. This is our duty toward this group of tomorrow's literati who hold the thread of our very existence in their hands, for tomorrow they will be an extension of us. We have to reconsider their position in the literary world; we who have come before them in the chain of time must question ourselves about what we have done for them and whether what we are going to do with them will have an effect on literature and its upcoming writers. First of all, we have to ask, do they really need us? What sort of help do they lack? Do they only need us to show that we care about their work? No doubt concern about an artist's work is the most important impetus for his enthusiasm. The artist is not eager to work for himself but works to hear an echo of his work; like a flower that thrives on the rays of the sun, the artist thrives on the tender look from the people. Whether these looks convey good or evil, the artist is not destroyed by criticism or abuse—on the contrary, they support his existence—but what actually destroys him is neglect. His coffin is nailed up and his grave is dug by forgetfulness. Artists who think their work has been neglected will start work on a different piece, entirely different from their previous one. These new works will often have nothing to do with literature or art. Therefore the world of art will be impoverished because these artists will just give up writing.

Therefore we should always bear in mind the work of artists and literary men and make them feel from time to time that their message is appreciated and is in our hearts and minds. We should also show them that we are grateful to them for their efforts and that we recognize their talents. But how do we achieve that? No doubt, we have a duty towards those who will follow us. We have been accused many times of being egoistic and unhelpful to others, and these accusations may be partly true, for sometimes we have been busy or occupied with other things, not, however, for love of ourselves but because we imagined that we were capable of shouldering the burden and taking on all responsibility for literature.

It might be a legitimate excuse for the work for we imagined that nothing would be completed except by our own hands. We worked hard for a long time and spent our life in forming, preparing, and completing the artistic goal as if it was incumbent only upon us to open up new fortresses and build palaces.

But life has taught us that we are only capable of building inroads and laying the foundations while others should get on with the building. Our feeling today is that we are like the man who begets a child in his old age! He is awakened suddenly and looks at things differently. He does not see himself as the center of the world, the sole bearer of the message, but he sees the world as a chain of links, each one a complement to the other. He realizes that his child has not been born in vain but is there to complete something that he is unable to complete. He has from that moment a task other than to reproduce: he has to support his offspring, help him to stand up so that he may shoulder his responsibilities.

The problem that always puzzles us is, how can we help? Can we help the new generation so that they will avoid our mistakes? Can we make them realize and come to terms with their own individual mistakes before their works are published? Or should the help come before the work is finished so they may be rectified? And what of those who have already achieved fame with their talents glittering like a twinkling star? Have we a duty towards them too? And if so, what is it? What is the means of fulfillment? We are all ready to perform our duty, and we will never refrain from performing this duty if we only know the way and the means of fulfilling it.

2

The Responsibilities of Every Generation

Every generation is responsible for its ideas that can pass on, knowingly or unknowingly, to the new generations. Therefore it is best to explain these ideas from time to time so as to avoid any misunderstanding.

For example, I have seen some young people move to Western countries seeking education and being struck by a different way of life and a foreign civilization, causing them to sometimes feel and think as Mohsen did in my book *Bird from the East* (1937), the day he traveled to the West after the first world war. They, like Mohsen, wander about there, looking for spirituality with one idea dominating their minds: the spirituality of the East, its greatness, its mores, and its origins. They then follow the other Mohsen in my other book *The Return of the Spirit* (1933), seeking, as he did, the source of their spiritual and cultural heritage, the traces of thousands of years deep within the conscience of Egypt, its countryside, and its honest inhabitants. They feel proud, as he did, of the genuineness of the Egyptian people and repeat his words praising their ancient civilization.

It is, of course, best to let young people live with such feelings and thoughts, but it is also best to say to them, honor your past, without going to extremes that would confine your spirit and not enable you to pursue everything new and of benefit to you, no matter how small it may be. Bravely serve yourself from every source and take from every heritage to enrich yourselves and broaden your horizons. This is a statement that I must always repeat.

There is danger for our future, every danger from that limited understanding of the words "our nature" and from this concept that makes our youth take from their Eastern spirituality and the traces of their Egyptian civilization prisons and fortresses isolating them from other ways of thinking in the world and preventing them from strongly and courageously contributing to general human intellectual activity. They should not look with alarm at Western culture or foreign civilizations, regarding them as demons easily capturing their souls. Our spirit is too strong and deep for another civilization to overwhelm it. So why have all this fear of facing other civilizations?

Anyone here who wishes to write a story wants to subtitle it clearly as an "Egyptian story" and is careful to make all the scenes in it take place on national territory, strongly imbued with local color. He does all the above to persuade himself that he is creating a national work of art that has a genuine Egyptian spirit. All this is a type of inferiority complex or unjustifiable fear. The genuine spirit of Egypt can be stamped on any subject it touches, even in foreign surroundings, just as the Islamic spirit could be stamped on architecture derived from that of the pagans and Byzantines, just as Shakespeare was able to personalize the legends he borrowed from the Italians, the Danes, and the people of the East.

A large part of great world literature deliberately takes for its subject matter countries and people foreign to it, fully confident that the foreign subject will not have the slightest effect on the distinctive character of its own literature. This strong self-confident literature puts its own stamp on the subjects it chooses and causes its national flag to flutter in whatever country it chooses.

Another idea needs to be elaborated. Some years ago, I published the following lines on page 105 of a book entitled *By the Light of the Green Lamp* (1942):

> The unveiling of women in Egypt preceded that of literature. That is why we see that a large part of our modern literature is still "imprisoned" and has the stuffy air of a closed room. A synthetic literature, a literature of "canned preservatives," of borrowed expressions, methods, and studies extracted from the stores of our ancestors. But the literature of fresh air, the literature of life pulsating with human emotions, literature that comes from the heart and addresses every heart on the face of the earth, that world literature that influences the spirit of every nation, every race, and every human being because it springs from the heart of a human being in a pure, true, and passionate form, that kind of literature we unfortunately have little of, because little is our share of frankness and honesty.

ꟹ

This subject has much been written about these days, as have the expressions "art and life," "art and emotion," "art and truthfulness," etc . . . which indicates that the significance of literature has taken a more fruitful direction in our contemporary society. But does this mean that we should stop reading the writings of our ancestors?

I regard it as my duty also to make something clear. The Ministry of Education commemorated Abul Ala al-Maari[1] and published his book *Saqt al-zand* (*The Tinder Spark*); so I applied myself to reading it again and emerged saying,

1. Abul Ala al-Maari (973–1058) was a celebrated Syrian philosopher and poet. *The Tinder Spark* was a collection of poems written around the late tenth century.

> The art of this genius is subject to a "double confinement." Is it an art of "fresh air," the heart, feeling, and life? Or is it the art of a blind man imprisoned in a closed room that truly brings us pleasure? But it is a pleasure that does not affect our emotions so much as it affects our thoughts, that does not move our hearts so much as it stirs our minds. We do not find pleasure easily in it, but we achieve it through our minds only after hard work, diligence, and deep thought.

So I should make clear to young people who read my general writings published some years ago that passionate feelings alone and the excitement they raise are not the whole of art nor the best of art sometimes, because pleasure that is acquired without plunging in deep is, most of the time, cheap. Werther's emotional pains are, in Goethe's view and that of the history of literature, inferior to Faust's mental anguish. The ambiguity of my previous statements is a result of my not explaining the meaning of "heart." "Heart" in art is truthfulness—not truthfulness in its limited sense restricted to that of emotion or sentiment but also truthfulness regarding a certain idea.

Accordingly, it is necessary to define the meaning of "life" in art. Undoubtedly, art is an expression of life, and it is not easy to imagine an art separated from life, unless we give the example of the art of Islamic decoration, which does not depict flowers, birds, or animals but is based on geometrical designs. It is undoubtedly an ancient and splendid art, but it is difficult to relate to the life that we know. This abstraction in Islamic decoration is similar to that in ancient Egyptian art whose broad lines were devoid of "flesh and blood" and whose main concern was to vivify an idea in stone, not to transform the stone to life as the Greeks did. Whichever type we prefer, the differences in mentalities, trends, and art oblige us to widen the meaning of "life" to include all these kinds of literature and art.

"Life" in art ought not to be only part of what is happening in the external world affecting man's senses and feelings, but should also be what is happening in the inner world, which man derives from his thoughts and contemplation. Life in literature and art is the whole of life, a complete life in its fullest sense, that life that lives in every part of the living human being, in his heart, his instinct, his senses, and his mind.

ᔕ

Such are some of the ideas we inadvertently left behind in books striving to enter young people's consciousness. How wonderful it would be if from time to time, either by our own hands or those of other critics and researchers, we could revise what we have published, recalling what we stated in order to provide new explanations, as banks do when they withdraw old bank notes from circulation and return them to the public in a new condition.

3

The Gap between the Generations

The relationship between generations is a natural phenomenon that always necessitates review, study, and research, but in Egypt it has taken some forms which give rise to amazement and bewilderment. I myself have experienced two extremely contradictory forms, the first being the relationship between our generation and the generation that preceded it. There is no need for me to describe it in words; it is sufficient to mention one incident that bears all the evidence and is of significance.

I heard my late father speak with deep respect about his father on all occasions. His father was one of those who, having studied at Al Azhar University,[1] then resided in the countryside, cultivating their own land. My father was in his late forties when he was promoted to the post of judge. His father continued to exercise his right to mortgage and sell his land, then buy and appropriate land, and then borrow money and make pledges and make contracts. Some friends said to him, "These are legal procedures, and your son is one of the best judges; haven't you consulted him?" The father only shouted, "My son? Do I consult children?"

1. Al Azhar University was founded in 970–972. It is the oldest degree-granting university in Egypt and the main center of Islamic learning in the world.

My father took no offence to this but received it with a smile of tolerance and respect for his father, though I believe that in his heart he did not think that his father was right. I never heard him criticize his father; he used to bend and kiss his hand whenever he met him and always found excuses for his father's behavior. He used to justify his many marriages by saying that whenever he married one woman, he found her more ignorant than the one before! As far as I remember, I imagined at that time that my father had a different point of view about the relationship that should bind father and son. However, something happened afterwards that greatly astonished and amazed me, for when I, in turn, reached my forties and joined the judiciary, I saw my father take one mortgage after another on a house we held dear to us. He used to meet with the brokers or usurers in front of me and would speak to them confidentially and whisper to them in their ears, and it never came to his mind to disclose to me what it was all about or what his purpose was. He never asked for my humble opinion about what he was about to do, though I investigated people's legal affairs every day, examined and weighed up all the pleas and evidence and bore the greatest responsibility for their lives, freedom, and property. Nevertheless I never even inwardly revolted, never raised my voice in his presence nor met him without kissing his hand even when I myself was old, and I always listened to his advice.

❧

This form of relationship, I believe, has disappeared with the passage of time, and another form of relationship has spread among the new generation who look at matters in a different way. They insist on having their say at home, school, and in society at large, for this generation lives in an age where the world situation justifies political coups d'état and national conditions call for freedom, finding in the previous generation that embraces it support and encouragement. For the previous generation was none other than that of the Egyptian Revolution. But our sons, who gained the right to express their opinions in all matters, did not stop at that, for no young man now accepts any advice, nor will you notice any respect for your age or your generation when he meets you. He addresses you as a peer whatever the difference may be in status or age. No young man nowadays is satisfied just to have a say regarding his family affairs, political ideologies, his university curricula, and his professors. To merely give his opinion is not enough for him.

The willfulness of youth, the confusion of ideas, the weakening of values, the convulsion of world events, and the speed of social developments have all made the new generation grow up with no respect for the old well-established and stable systems, ideas, values, and figures. With the collapse of this wall, the youth were free to wander in every valley without control with one firm belief in their heads, namely, that there is no other opinion but their own to set matters right and that they have the right to impose their opinions on their parents, professors, and leaders whenever they can.

❧

In these two forms of relationship lies the gap between the generations. In the past, our parents imposed their will on us; in the present, we see that our children want to impose their will on us! Are we, then, the generation without a will? We gave it to our parents out of deference, and we have given it to our sons for encouragement!

4

The Clash of Generations

Whenever there is a gap between generations in a society, each generation is of the opinion that the society is alien to it, that it is not to be blamed for it, that it does not know how it came to be nor who is responsible for it. I have received two letters representing these two different views of society.

The first, which represents the viewpoint of the older generation, runs as follows:

> Our generation had night clubs, the "Casino de Paris" and the young ladies of the "Orchestre Café Egyptien" for the Europeanized class, and two cafés for dance and song in "Wagh el Berka," but today it has become one of the requisites of the middle class to have American bars in their private homes. It has also become the right of my neighbor to use a loudspeaker to get on my nerves. Effeminate men walk hand in hand on the pavements! Everything is topsy-turvy. The Law dreads crime; the father is apprehensive of the revolt of his son who has been nursed by a licentious sort of freedom! But outside Egypt, the law governs the society. One day a leading Egyptian actress who was sitting cross-legged in a tram in Genoa was obliged to uncross her legs. She protested, regarding the law as restricting her freedom, but in the end she was obliged to abide by the laws of the society in which she was living, though she did so reluctantly.

As for the new generation, it is represented in the following letter:

> As a member of the new generation, I say, it is a generation that desires to understand the meaning of life to the greatest possible degree with regard to knowledge, progress, and refinement. This in spite of what is noted in this generation's behavior, as regards recklessness and impulsiveness unchecked by reason and understanding, so that people are apprehensive of its actions, which they consider dangerous for this new generation and for society. No doubt the new generation has made mistakes, but on whom does the responsibility fall? Is it not the older generation that is responsible? For the older generation did not know how to lead the new generation to a safe harbor. It was frightened by the sudden development in human thought and gave the new generation free rein to act. It could not decide whether to go forward with the new generation or to step out of the way. Here lies its hesitation and failure. Or did it ignore or overlook the developments in public life, and want to make the new generation move backwards? The result was, in all cases, that the older generation failed to do so because our contemporary life does not allow any living person to go backwards, for if he does, he will be crushed under the wheels of progress. The disparity lies in the difference between the natures of the two generations: one wants to proceed slowly, the other wants to leap. This is nothing new.

This has always been the case between fathers and sons in all places and times. But what is new in our contemporary age—the age of revolutions and coups d'état—is that the difference in the nature and the viewpoints of the two generations turned into a revolution, one that has diverse aspects to it: at home, in the school, in the workplace and society. It was no longer easy to differentiate between the boundaries of discipline and freedom, right and duty. Thus destinies were all mixed up, values were lost, the relationship between the generations was damaged and the links between them were severed. Cooperation between the two generations ended, and the state of affairs became what we now see, with each generation suspicious of the other.

The crisis, then, lies in this gap between the generations. Sons revolted against their parents and subjects revolted against their leaders. In the two points of view, there is a rejection of the state of society and recognition that it is based on corruption. What is important now is not to cast blame or level accusations, but to find where the weakness lies and find the cure. Undoubtedly new ways of thinking are developing fast, life is being renewed, and society is obliged to follow all this in spite of itself, like a piece of paper borne along with the current. I doubt that many of the older generation would think of stopping the wheel of time or of turning back the clock, although they are sometimes accused of being swept along by the current without building any bridges or dams. For the comprehensive renovation of aspects of society is not in fact accomplished without the inspiration, consent, and forbearance of the older generation.

But the new generation lives in the age of rapid changes, swift developments and amazing inventions. That is why it has become less patient and persevering than the previous generation, stronger in the desire for change, and more violent in its revolt against everything that is fixed and stable. In truth, the disagreement between the two generations does not lie in the principles of development and innovation, for all would agree on the need for innovation and development. The real disagreement in this clash lies in the lack of respect and trust, and the adoption not of an attitude of cooperation but one of challenge.

5

The Mutual Disregard between the Generations

The breaking of the link between the generations also results from ignorance of the nature of each generation and disregard for each other's needs. The following is a letter that depicts the mutual disregard on the part of the two generations:

> My father prevents me from reading magazines or newspapers of all kinds and does not accept any discussion about the benefits of reading, and whenever he sees a magazine in my hands, he tears it up! He forbids me to make friends, even if they are cultured. He is suspicious of everything that I do and is always worrying about me. He wants me to live like a worshiper in a hermitage, with no one allowed to see me or I them. I am passionate about reading, so what can I do, in order to practice my hobby and at the same time please my father for whom I have the greatest respect?

This is the kind of father who wants to raise his son like a flower that grows only in greenhouses. I am not an expert on education or a botanist who can debate this issue, but I believe that any human being or plant that is not exposed to the sun, air, wind, and dust will grow to be delicate and weak and will need to be wrapped in care in order to survive, and surrounded by a wall of precautions in order to live. Once a hole is made in this armor this entity will wither at the first touch! No, fearful parent, this is not the way to behave; smash the greenhouse and take out your flower, expose it tenderly to the sun and air. Let your son read, make friends, and live the spring of his life.

Do not fear the kind of books your son reads at this early age. Nature is wiser than you are, O father. It is nature that nurtures personal inclinations and colors them according to age as it gives color to the leaves on the trees. In youth, imagination, feeling, and passion blossom, while in old age reason, wisdom, and experience blossom. It is wrong for a father to challenge nature and impose his will on it and expect at an early age a tree that is straight and strongly built while exposed to the rough wind. However, this seems to be the story of every father who wants to control his son according to his own liking, and takes his temperature with a thermometer. It is as if he is incapable of understanding him just as the winter is incapable of understanding spring and mocks at its pure white flowers on the pliant green branches and ridicules its singing birds, moonlit nights, sweet scented breeze, and all the tenderness with which spring fills the world. That tender spring season! From harsh winter's point of view, this tenderness is weakness because winter is the season of violence in which the elements are in conflict and forces contend with each other. It is life in its greatest struggle.

I was involved in a similar situation with my late father—God have mercy upon him—when I was twelve years of age. I was scared of Fridays because that was the day when my father had more time to spend with me to discuss what I was reading and choose the books he thought I should read. One of the least difficult among the books that he chose was *The Seven Mu'allaqat.*[1] Because of this book, I received the most painful

1. *The Seven Mu'allaqat* is a collection of the finest pre-Islamic Arabic poems that were hung on the walls of AlKabbah.

of beatings, for my father was not satisfied with my learning the poems by heart but also wanted me to explain these difficult pre-Islamic verses to him at such a young age. When I was unable to do so, he would wonder at my ignorance and stupidity and become furious, motivated no doubt by anxiety about my future. He would slap my face until my nose started to bleed and shout at me, "You ignorant boy! You stupid boy! Is there anything easier than this verse by Zuhair Ibn Abi Salma?[2] This is a very easy and enjoyable verse, you fool! 'And he, who does not work hard at many things / will be bitten by fangs and trampled underfoot by horses.'" He would then shake his head admiringly at the wisdom in the verse. It is true that this verse was worthy of appreciation by my father because he knew through experience the truth of every word in these lines. But what amazes me now is this: How could my father not understand that the mind of a twelve-year-old could not grasp the truth of that verse?

Was I expected to repeat a rote explanation of the verse as I recited it by heart? What was the use of that? It would make me little better than a parrot. What was meant, I believe, was that one should explain the meaning of the verse with sincerity, with all one's feelings, understanding, and personal knowledge of what was being explained. In that case, a boy or youth should be asked to explain the verse only according to what his life experience enables him to understand and feel.

Therefore, both the father and the school should make sure that the boy or youth is not subjected to this kind of self-deception or deception of others by teaching him "ready-made" explanations of things that his age cannot enable him

2. Zuhair Ibn Abi Salma was one of the finest poets in pre-Islamic times.

to understand. For that reason too, it is better for the father and the school to make it possible for the boy or youth to read material that is suitable for his age.

Do not worry, O father, and do not think that your son—now immersed in these facile and trivial reading materials—will continue to be drawn by that current until the end of his life.

The current of life is what changes the type of readings. You yourself, O father—who now read philosophical works and political and economic articles, who praise history, the finest literature, psychology, or mathematics—used as a boy to be an avid reader of the stories of Rocambole and Abu Zayd Al-Hilali.[3] But, like most fathers, you do not remember that phase. You imagine that you have never read a story because your life today draws you away from the life of the imagination, and it seems to you that your mind can no longer bear to digest such stories! O father! Let your son be his age. Try to understand his generation.

3. Rocambole is a fictional adventurer. He is the invention of the nineteenth-century French writer Pierre du Terrail. Abu Zayd Al-Hilali was an eleventh-century Arab leader and hero of the Amirid tribe of Banu Hilal. In Egyptian culture, he is well known for his many chivalrous adventures.

6

Deprived Children

How happy we were with the advent of the month of Ramadan[1] in our wonderful childhood and how anguished we also felt!

Who can forget the beating of one's little heart in childhood as one stood in front of the lantern store, to gaze with wondering eyes at the various lanterns of colored glass?

How splendid that lantern looks that is suspended there, with its yellow, green, and red! It is undoubtedly expensive. Will the parents be willing to make such a sacrifice for their child? In any case, it will not cost them too much but will fill their child's heart with joy, the extent of which adults can never fully appreciate. How cruel grownups sometimes are! They may begrudge spending a few dirhams that they will not miss, which is the difference between one toy and another. But in actual fact, it will make the difference between one kind of happiness and another. How forgetful grownups are that they were all young once. Why can't they remember that wonderful magical world that suddenly opens its golden gates to children whenever they desire to acquire one of the things they dream

1. Ramadan is the month when Muslims fast from dawn to sunset every day. In Egypt, parents buy lanterns for their children to play with and sing songs as they swing their lanterns.

about? It is a world of heavenly bliss in which none but they can live for such a low price.

If only grownups would remember that world whose gates were closed to them as soon as they left the world of childhood, then they would not deprive their children of anything. Now that they have the power in their hands and the money in their pockets, they will be unable to make the smallest opening into that world even if they offer their fortune and their lives. How wonderful is that miracle called childhood. In it you can enter a paradise—which you will never enter again—for a few piasters. Ask all the millionaires in any nation: can you buy today, with all your millions, a moment of happiness like that which you bought in your childhood for a dirham or two?

Do you see how your millions dwindle when compared to a child's fortune? Your gold turns into dust when compared with the treasures of childhood.

Yet there is a problem that requires thought and deliberation: if you were able to satisfy your child's needs and fulfill his dreams, would you do so or not? Is it in the child's interests to fulfill all his desires or to keep some of his desires unfulfilled?

I mention this because in my childhood I did not get all the toys or things that I longed to have. Therefore I had to create them in my rich imagination. Some of my peers and neighbors possessed precious and wonderful toys that filled their rooms and filled me with wonder. I stood among these toys in amazement; I gazed at them admiringly and touched them, saying, "Allah is great!" Meanwhile their owner would toy with them, breaking them and treating them with contempt. Undoubtedly I knew their worth more than he did and saw in them splendid things that his eyes were unable to see. It was as if every screw, puzzle, or key in them stirred my imagination and my senses. That was because I did not own them and could not acquire them.

What would education specialists advise parents to do in raising up their child? Fulfill his needs or turn a deaf ear to some of his demands? Should he be given the joy of possession or be made to taste the bitterness of deprivation? Thus with the arrival of Ramadan when the child looks longingly at the colorful decorative lantern hanging in the shop, the question is, would you leave his imagination to cling to it and his dreams to swing with it, and buy him another, or would you buy the lantern of his choice, light its candle, satisfy his imagination and ardor, and put an end to his anguish?

7

The Making of the Generations

An American biologist believes that in the next five years every couple will be able to choose the sex of the child they want. Whoever wants a boy will have a boy and whoever wants a girl will have a girl.

Knowledge wants to hand human beings a terrible key from among those of wise nature. Knowledge! It is the desire that abides in human beings' minds and drives them to possess what they should not. It is as if Mother Nature, this merciful mother catching sight of her child's hand stretching out to her pillow to pull the key out from under it, rises and says to herself, filled with misgiving and anxiety,

> You fool! Do you want to manage all your affairs on your own? I am afraid you may not be capable nor worthy of this. I am the one who runs your life free of all your whims, rising above your pettiness. I view your destiny not in its limited individuality but in connection with the destiny of other living creatures. You will regret such rashness someday.

It is as if the human being addresses Mother Nature in the name of science: "I am no longer a child and since I have found your key, I am worthy of taking and using it!" And Mother Nature whispers:

> All children say that and take the key to open forbidden safes to look for candy or pleasure, but they scatter the

contents and cause disorder! Do as you please and we shall see what will happen.

❧

Only one thing can happen: when people discover that they can choose a boy and all they have to do is take a dose of medicine for a little money, they will rush in droves to the pharmacies to buy the medicine that will make them beget boys. One generation later, we shall find the world filled with males.

Then a global problem will ensue: the search for females. Wars and battles may break out among men for the sake of women, as the Trojan wars broke out for Helen.

At this point the situation will be reversed, and people will rush anew to pharmacies to purchase the other medicine in order to beget females. Only one generation later we shall find the world full of women!

Then the problem of finding men will ensue; the stampede to storehouses and pharmacies will recur, and so on and so forth until some sort of balance is achieved a few generations later.

Thus this big child is unable to achieve a balance in his personal affairs without a great cost in effort, and after a long time of muddling between extremes and swinging between opposites.

❧

This assumption is based on the good intentions of Man and his ability ultimately to control his whims and replace "Nature" in organizing his faculties. But there is another assumption that is based on man's inability and failure. Then it is inevitable for Nature to intervene. This patient and alert mother cannot be forbearing and lenient to the point of negligence! Therefore, no sooner does she perceive her child's tomfoolery reaching the point of breaking her rules than she rushes to him and takes matters into her hands to set them right and restore the balance in her own way.

If the number of males becomes excessive with no possible way to correct the imbalance, Nature will awaken strife and launch wars that will cut down the excess of this crop. And if the females outnumber the males, Nature will spread promiscuity, epidemics, and social revolutions whose waves will wipe out the excessive numbers that have to be eliminated.

Only then will Nature achieve victory and become certain that man has learned this lesson. She only wants him to be aware of his arrogance, admit his rashness, and listen to her whisper as she bends over him with a forgiving and compassionate smile:

"Have you played enough? Wouldn't it be better now, my son, to let me manage your affairs?"

8

Nature's Generations

The Chinese thinker Yutang[1] states,

> There are some people who refuse to produce offspring! Can trees or flowers refuse to produce seeds that ensure the continuation of their species? The problem of this age is that many people do not marry, and many who do get married refuse to reproduce for various reasons: such as rising living standards, the rise in the cost of living, and the hardships of earning a living.

Not one of the above reasons—according to him—should prevent mankind from performing their natural duty like a tree or flower.

That is true! However, in my opinion there is a difference between a tree or flower and a human being. The tree would not consider opposing the laws of Nature. It would never forget that it is part of Nature itself and that when it produces seeds it leaves to life the task of sorting the good from the bad. It also does not rush the outcome; it lets time work freely for species to grow or die, sacrificing hundreds of thousands or billions to eventually produce the perfect species.

1. Lin Yutang (1895–1976) was a Chinese writer, linguist, translator, and inventor. He produced many best-sellers in the United States, where he lived from 1935 on, about Chinese philosophy.

It is different for the human being. He is a thinking animal or a plant that reasons. The function of the mind and of thought is to formulate principles and laws, and these laws and principles often contradict the laws of Nature. That is because the rational human being formulates his principles within the limited framework of his time. On the other hand, Nature forms its own principles within the limitless framework of its time. Most of the time, it is from this that the misunderstanding between Nature and human beings springs. Most of the people who do not marry have made that decision based on one of the principles of the mind that makes the idea of individual freedom attractive as a picture of human happiness.

This man who is as free as a bird—without a nest anywhere—is not afraid of tomorrow and challenges adversity. How happy he is in his solitary state, peace of mind, and lack of responsibilities! All his life he flaps his wings without sheltering anybody with them, until he dies of cold without a nest or goes on in life satisfied and without any regrets. Thus does the mind gain victory over Nature.

The bird may feel that flying does not bring him freedom but rather a sense of loss, and that his happiness does not lie in spreading his wings in the air but in spreading them over a nest and a mate. Only then does Nature triumph over the mind and man weds. But his mind will not let him be; it goes back to laying down its principles and establishing laws, saying, "Your income is small so do not beget children, or have just one child!" or "Your income is average so have two children." Man listens to the laws of his mind and not to the laws of Nature.

The law of his mind wants to connect the income with offspring, while the law of Nature does not see a connection between them. The limited law of the mind wants to confine the number of offspring within the framework of the shortness of human time and the limits of living expenses.

As for Nature's mind—which is boundless—it does not expect the results of this procreation until generations later when countries succeed one another and systems change.

The secret lies in the fact that primitive human beings by instinct produce many offspring while the educated ones beget less. The former is more resistant to his mind, more in harmony with Nature and more obedient to its laws, whereas the latter is more resistant to Nature and more obedient to his mind.

The words of the Chinese thinker apply only to primitive man. He alone is like a tree or a flower that reproduces without thought, and Nature has to sort out the good and the bad of his offspring to keep the strong and destroy the weak while he submissively accepts her verdict.

As for the educated man, he does not accept Nature's verdict concerning his offspring. He wants to be the one to decide their fate and consequently directs them in life to a program of his own making and drawn up by his mind.

It is thus a war between educated thinking human beings and Nature. And so long as civilization turns every man into an educated thinking individual, the gap of disparity between Nature and Man will widen to the extent that the progeny will increase or decrease according to an official program designed by the state and applied to its citizens.

The way out of this problem is through wisdom. If man is given wisdom, he will hold the scales that enable him to make a balance between his will and that of Nature to ensure his success.

9

The Diversity of Generations

In the Sura Hud of the holy Koran is a verse whose meaning is understood by few: "If thy Lord had so willed, He could have made mankind one people, but they will not cease to dispute."[1]

Whatever the interpretations that have been made of this verse, I seem to see a gleam of light inside it that may be associated with God's way in creating the world.

The difference in the size of the planets is the secret behind their gravity, connectivity, and cooperation. Had God made the planets of the same size and similar in all their elements, weights, and features, they would have lost their connectivity and fallen out of their galaxies.

As for our planet and its inhabitants, this law of diversity is just as necessary. I recently read the work of the English thinker John Hadham,[2] and it seemed to me as if he was inspired by the aforesaid Koranic verse when he wrote,

> If every country had the same features and raw materials as the rest of the other countries, each would have been totally independent from its neighbours. But God organized the

1. From Abdullah Yusuf Ali's interpretation of the Koran. Beirut: Dar Al-fikr, n.d.

2. John Hadham wrote various books such as *God in a World War* (1940), *Between God and Man* (1942), and *God and Human Progress* (1944).

world map so that every country would be to a great or small extent in need of every other country.

This statement also applies to nations, for every nation has been granted an advantage that can be a contribution to all of the nations. And every nation owes the other nations something that they need in their production or lack in their composition.

What applies to nations applies to individuals who form the nation. Every well-structured society is built on the diversity of its individuals in the kind of work they perform and in their ways of thinking. A healthy community is one that is built upon the contribution to this community that every individual makes in his own field of work, his personal experience, his temperament, which is different from that of others, his nature and his outlook. Can you imagine a society made up of individuals who are all pessimistic in their outlook or all optimistic, all prudent or all negligent, all poets, all engineers, or all preachers?

∽

If we want to complete the picture, let us take the organs in a human being. A healthy body is also based on this difference in the functions of the organs: the brain thinks, the heart feels, the tongue speaks, the ear hears, and the foot walks. Our health would deteriorate the day we see all these organs abandon their various functions and adopt just one function for all, namely, thinking. Yes, what would happen to the body if the heart, tongue, ear, and foot rebelled and all said, "We will not feel, talk, hear, or walk? We all want to be like the brain and not do anything but think." This would undoubtedly mean total paralysis of the body and its collapse, inability to move, speak, or feel, and thinking alone would be of no use to it.

God's way in creation is apparent in this diversity in attributes, forms, and distinguishing features. Here lies the secret of symmetry in creation, in other words, the secret of its solidarity: the organs work together cooperatively because they have different functions, for if they had similar functions they would not have collaborated and each organ would immediately have become independent, and such independence would make the body fall apart and the individual would crumble.

❧

If we move to the sphere of opinion, we shall perceive that having different points of view in human society is a natural necessity, namely, a phenomenon of God's will. There is a difference between having different opinions and having different mentalities. Two people may have similar mentalities but different opinions.

A sound society must be founded on unity and harmony in the mentality of its people, its generations, and its general characteristics, without this affecting their different opinions. Our human arrogance should not make us assume that only the ideas we have in our heads should be accepted by everybody else. No one opinion can prevail in this world.

The world today is divided into two camps and two world views; each one wants to efface the other: capitalism on one side and communism on the other. Each is making from the atom a bomb to wipe out its rival from the map of the world. A decisive war may break out between them sooner or later.

But what will not happen is that the world will agree on one point of view, even if one of the two sides achieves a sweeping and devastating victory. No sooner would the victorious side win than they would immediately have different and conflicting points of view. And so on and so forth! For such is the Creator's eternal plan: "If thy Lord had so willed, He could have made mankind one people, but they will not cease to dispute."

10

The Principle of the Coming Generations

The world is a brightly colored carriage with gold borders—drawn by beautiful horses—driven by the devil.

This glib coachman always knows how to address the passengers. He knows well how people love goodness or pretend to love it and avoids addressing them with his real tongue. He has invented a new language for them that is skillful, glittering, and filled with nobility and sublimity.

He bows at the door of the carriage, his forehead nearly touching the ground in humility, then opens the door, and says to the people, "Ascend, please, so I can give you a lift to the noblest of destinations."

Some of them step in: the believers, those with a motive, and the aimless.

The believer says to himself, "All is well with the world. I thank God that He has provided us with this kind coachman to take us to what we believe to be a noble destination."

The motivated passenger says to himself, "I don't care where the coachman takes us but what I care about is to be next to these noble believers."

The implicated one says to himself, "I didn't intend to ride in the carriage, but as long as all the people around me are getting on with this coachman, why should I stay behind?"

The coachman closes the door of the carriage with a smile, jumps into the driver's seat, takes hold of the reins, and whips the horses. The carriage sets off, madly racing the wind.

❧

A little later the passengers begin to feel a violent rocking that almost destroys the carriage, makes them dizzy, and throws them against one another. When they look out of the window, they discover that the driver has left the even roads, deviated from the straight lanes, and has descended into rough and muddy paths.

The believers cry out in horror, "Woe upon you! What is this path you are taking us along?"

Turning towards them, the driver says with concealed cunning, "It is the shortest route!"

The believers reply, "But it is not clean!"

The coachman retorts, "What matters is the destination you are heading to. Since your destination is noble, don't pay attention to the road!"

He resumes whipping the horses and the carriage rushes to its destination, leaving the believers inside looking at one another and asking, "Must we really take these muddy paths to reach our noble destination?"

The nonbelievers, who keep up appearances, and the implicated, take part in this conversation, saying, "If this is the shortest path, what is the harm?"

This silences the believers, and they resign their lot to God; but in actual fact they have but resigned it to the devil!

❧

This has long been the carriage of life since everyone adopted the principle, "The end justifies the means." This is the most dangerous principle known to the successive generations of mankind. This principle alone is responsible for all the disasters that have befallen the world, generation after generation, to this day.

All the world's politicians and leaders, in the past and the present—and undoubtedly in the future—have followed this principle. They have been deceived into thinking that it is the shortest path to reach their ends, which may sometimes be noble, but what always happens is the same as what happens to the carriage driven by the devil. They take only muddy paths and their destination never appears before them on the horizon.

That is because the dirty winding path never leads to anything good or honorable! Noble objectives are not so base as to accept being reached through ignoble means. The path to honor is nothing but honor itself.

Good is in itself the means and the end because it is one of the rays of God. And God Almighty is an end whose path must be that of light and good.

If leaders of the world meeting around tables of peace as well as leaders of nations, societies, and intellectuals seeking the future of mankind first agree to destroy the principle of "the end justifies the means," the results will be impressive. Only then will politicians' maneuvers disappear and lying, evasion, hypocrisy, and deceit cease. Only one clear and clean path will remain for everybody. If it leads us up to the general good that will be the goal and if it does not lead to speedy reform the world will at least have trodden a path devoid of evil and mire. If that clean path is not one of reform and good, the world will never know reform and good through the path of destruction and evil.

Can we hope that in the new generations a new principle will evolve? A principle that the whole world can take as an article of faith and a doctrine whose motto will be, "Noble ends are reached by noble means!"

11

The Ghost of a Generation

I went to Rue Pelleport in the suburb of Paris—where I used to live after World War I—and what did I find? I found the narrow street just as it used to be, and my room just as it used to be, with its open window overlooking the wide empty space. I admit that I was touched, and a shiver ran through me as I imagined I saw somebody at the window, somebody I once knew: a slim young man with black hair looking at the distant horizon as if he wanted to rend the veil of the unknown to read the tablet of his destiny. But destiny—it seemed—had not inscribed one letter on the tablet. Destiny was waiting for the young man to inscribe what he wanted to do with his life. Yes, the young man had drawn a sort of map for his life, a clear and detailed one. He had abandoned the legal profession in Egypt to take up the pen and write in order to tell people things that he believed might be useful to them. He did not want anything else nor desire more for his life; for power did not seduce him, nor did the temptations of life appeal to him, nor did wealth attract or satisfy him.

Sometimes when a person sets a plan for his life, destiny takes it and implements it.

Accordingly, "Destiny" approached the young man, received the plan and transferred it to the tablet, whispering with a smile, "Since you are the 'architect' who has meticulously designed his life, I will be the honest contractor."

The contractor kept his promise, finished the work, and constructed the building in accordance with the design, no more, no less.

ᘓ

I wished I could ask the young man whom I imagined standing at the window, "Do you like that building?"

Of course I did not receive an answer from the young man. Nor did I know what he could have said at his age. But I heard the answer from deep within me: "No . . . I do not like it!"

I then imagined I heard Destiny say sarcastically, "It is not my fault. I executed what I was given. If there is a fault it is in the design."

I immediately said, "Don't worry. No one is blaming you! Undoubtedly the one to blame is the inexperienced architect."

He proudly stated, "When it is left to me to make the design, I create miracles."

Thereupon I said, "Of course. But what do you say about those inexperienced architects who draw plans, imprisoning themselves in an imaginary design from which they cannot escape till the end of time?"

He said, "No matter how imaginative a human being is, he cannot surpass my imagination. I can show you ten people you know who are today millionaires; one of whom was a truck driver, another a street vendor of miscellaneous small wares, a third a worker in a fruit store, and so forth. Not one of them drew up a plan for his life or imagined a drawing of his destiny. They all left it to me to design and construct their lives, so I did for them what they never thought of doing."

I said, "What did you do for them?"

"I built their lives on pillars of gold."

"Did you give them money?"

"Yes, I drowned them in money."

"Yes, you drowned them!" I said this in a whisper, shaking my head slowly, in a way that implied sarcasm.

Destiny said, "What do you mean? Didn't I give them more than they expected?"

I promptly replied, "That is true, because they didn't expect more than that from life."

He slyly said, "What more is there in life than that?"

I smilingly said, "Don't you know?"

He said, "Do you know of a brighter light than the glitter of gold?"

I immediately responded, "Small hearts are lit by gold, but big hearts cannot be lit by mountains of gold!"

He said, "Then I am, in your point of view, nothing but a cheap architect and contractor."

I said, "You are an architect and a contractor accustomed to designing and building small houses. Now I realize that big houses are only designed by their owners."

He slyly remarked, "Why then did you complain just now of the structure of your life?"

I instantly said, "Because the young man who drew the design was well intentioned and had a vivid imagination. He drew in his mind a large house . . . so large that I could not fill it nor feel at home in it. I was imprisoned in a spacious palace whose halls and parlors neither my faith nor my efforts nor my abilities could fill."

ꕥ

Having said this, I left Rue Pelleport after casting a last glance at the ghost, of the young man standing at the window. I whispered, "Goodbye! Sorry I could not do more than that. Perhaps you were overoptimistic."

I walked in the street where the market was held every week from which the young man used to carry away his provisions such as rice and eggs, making the few francs that he had last the whole month. But he was happy, as it is not just food that helps man to survive. Yes, he was happy with the hope that shone on the horizon as if it were a star.

Nothing had changed in that distant quarter, except the star that had disappeared and the horizon that was now veiled in mist.

12

Between Two Generations

One morning, a young writer visited me and presented me with an Egyptian novel he had written and published. He was proud and invigorated like a tree bearing fruit. So I held his novel carefully and tenderly in my hand, read the title, and started to turn a few pages. There was a movement at the door. I looked up and beheld a good-looking, elegantly dressed young woman with a bright face and forehead, who asked to come in. She entered and sat down without giving me a chance to reply. Not waiting for me to speak, she quickly said clearly and steadily, "I am a disappointed and vexed reader . . . I came to ask you one question: What are you doing now? Years have passed since you last published a book. Is it journalism that has kept you busy?" She indicated with a movement of her hand to the busy noisy atmosphere around my desk.

I turned to her to reply, but the young man was quicker than I, crying enthusiastically, "Must he write and publish books? Do no other books worth reading appear from time to time?"

The girl glanced at him in astonishment and looked at me questioningly. She found me nodding my head in agreement. She turned back to the young man and said, "I am asking him what is keeping him busy."

The young man replied forcefully and impetuously, "It is none of our business! He may busy himself with anything that pleases him, which is better than filling two or three hundred pages of a story to be presented every season so that it would be said that he published his works regularly. It would be easy for him to repeat himself. He could have published endless works that resembled *Return of the Spirit*, *Bird from the East*, *The Sacred Bond*, and *Social and Intellectual Plays*, or he could make use of history books from which to adapt endless stories and publish every season what you and others like you want, merely for the sake of publication or profit, or to make his presence felt or to show that he is working energetically."

"Do you think that he scorns doing that? Or that he considers it useless?" she enquired.

"You should ask him. Here he is in front of you!"

❧

The girl looked at me for a moment then despairingly turned to the young man. "He keeps shaking his head. You answer!"

"Why should I speak for him? And why do you insist on talking about him? If you wish, I could talk to you about myself. I undoubtedly know all the details. I am a writer and a novelist and . . ."

"How remarkable! But I did not come to speak to you."

"Young lady, that is where you are mistaken! If I were you, I would have immediately asked who that gifted young man was who so boldly entered the conversation. Would ask him to come and talk to me about his recently published book so that I could be assured that literature is doing well, regardless of whether the owner of this room writes or not, whether he publishes books or not, or whether he lives or not."

"It was really courageous or even bold of you to interfere in such a way."

"Don't look at the 'occupant of the room'! He will not come to your rescue. He won't talk, and he won't give his opinion. As you've seen, he will only reply with a shake of the head."

"That is true! Have you known him long?"

"I have known him for fifteen years. I was fifteen years old when my family at home discussed *Return of the Spirit*, but I didn't care to read it until I was twenty. At that time, I grew up with many of my peers at university, discussing that long Egyptian novel that broke new ground. They swore with youthful enthusiasm that they would continue on that same path and would one day produce similar or better novels about our national life. Some fulfilled their promise by publishing stories that were to a great extent humorous and well written. I can assure you, miss, that I am one of those geniuses. I say it both frankly and humbly."

"I am sure of your frankness and humility. In any case, rest assured that I am beginning to be interested in your work. But first won't you let me know a little about the matter that brought me here today."

"Go ahead! What do you want to know?"

"The question of course is not directed to you. I wanted to know how he could abandon his refined art and condescend to write for newspapers."

"For heaven's sake! You all have perplexed him! If he rises with his art to higher planes, you would say why doesn't he descend to the people, feel what they are feeling, and study their lives, acquaint himself with their news, present their complaints, and defend their rights? And if he did that, you would say, 'Where is the isolation of the writer that will allow him to write for the elite?' My advice to you, miss, is that you should not ask these silly questions. Forgive me! The person who writes for hundreds of thousands and can be of some use and help them to rise a little is a man doing a public service!"

"What about his art?"

"No artist can neglect his art even if he wants to. Maybe you are confused between art and the production of books every season! You have confused the artist and teacher with the producer and merchant. What do you call somebody who remains silent when he should be silent for two, three, five, or ten years, to study himself anew, weigh his thoughts, store his experiences, observe the lives of the people and the developments in the society, and to revise our old works and search silently and patiently for new ways of artistic expression? Publication is easy, miss, but what is difficult is the long search in darkness. Maybe you will find him now busy searching for a kind of art that has nothing whatsoever to do with what he has tackled so far. 'Art is eternal, and life is short'—these are Goethe's well-known words. Whoever wants to hold on to art in his limited life span has to skip over unnecessary repetition and run after his mirage in every path until the grave."

The young man stopped talking and looked at me as if to inquire "Am I right?" He too received a nod from me.

As for the girl, she approved of the young writer's words, saying, "Allow me to express my admiration of your understanding of art and inquire about your book. I'm eager to read it. In which bookstore can I find it?"

"I'm very sorry, miss. I came here with only one copy but if you allow me to escort you now to the nearest bookstore, I'll present you with a signed copy. Do you have anything else to keep you here?"

"There is no need for me to stay; we can go instantly." She stood up, hastily bade me farewell, and left. The young man stood up to follow her after also taking hurried leave of me. No sooner had he reached the threshold of the door than an idea occurred to him; he retraced his footsteps and came close to me, whispering imploringly, "The bookstores are now closed. I would be very grateful if you would kindly return this copy to me so I can give it to her now. I'll bring you another copy later. The future is more important than the past!"

The only thing I could do was to hand him the copy, winking at him and smiling with approval. "You are right! And I see that the future is bright and clear!"

13

The Coming Together of Generations

I never imagined that I would deal with such a subject. However, it seemed to me possible when I began to look at it from a different perspective. It became no longer about merely a father–son relationship. It transcended that narrow framework to a wider and larger one: it was the picture of the relationship between the generations in our present age. I remembered an article I had published concerning this subject over twenty years ago, and on reviewing it, I found to my surprise that it was entitled "The Gap Between the Generations." I stated that the new generation

> insist[s] on having their say at home, school, and in society at large, for this generation lives in an age where the world situation justifies political coups d'état and national conditions call for freedom, finding in the previous generation that embraces it support and encouragement. For the previous generation was none other than that of the Egyptian Revolution of 1919. But our sons did not stop at that, for no young man now accepts any advice. . . . No young man nowadays is satisfied just to have a say regarding his family affairs, political ideologies, his university curricula, and his professors.

The new generation lives in an age characterized by rapid changes, speedy developments, and surprising inventions.

Therefore he has less patience and less stamina than the previous generation but has a stronger desire for change, and a fiercer rebelliousness against anything that is stable and fixed. The real point of controversy in the clash between generations is the loss of respect and trust and their acting not in the spirit of cooperation but with an attitude of challenge.

These words date back to 1947–1948. Man, of course, had not yet landed on the moon. Nor had he experienced loss of gravity, nor walked upside down in outer space. Do you think that things have changed between generations? Today I am the father of a son who represents the new generation, a generation that is over twenty years of age and not yet thirty. With a gap of three generations between us, what kind of dialogue can ensue? How cooperative should I be with him? My father did not know much about me, including the most important aspect in my life, which is art. I did not dare to utter the word "art" in his presence. If I had to mention it, I would have to use a more acceptable and respectful word, namely, "literature." In spite of that, as soon as he heard of my connection with literature—although I had graduated from the faculty of law—he would ask for God's forgiveness and become overwhelmed with unease and worry. Whenever I happened to meet a friend of his, he would say, "Your father is complaining in dismay to everybody that the craft of art has entrapped his son!" Now that I am devoted to art and literature, fate has decreed that I have a son who also wants to be affiliated to one of the crafts of art! Has the situation changed?

If you asked my son, he would say that nothing has changed, for he feels the same gap that I felt with my own father. He has not said this directly to me, out of courtesy, but his opinion was conveyed to me. I kept asking myself, how can this happen to someone like me and in this day and age? I kept analyzing the situation to discover where the fault lay.

Was it the result of my total disregard of the artistic path he has chosen? Perhaps! For the idea has become deeply embedded in his mind for quite some time now that I am not enthusiastic about what he is doing and that I would have preferred that he kept away from art. I do not know how this idea came about. He may have deduced it from a number of signs that began with my concern ever since he was young to direct him to become an engineer. He proceeded in that direction with his outstanding excellence in mathematics until he took me by surprise when he suddenly showed artistic tendencies before his final year of prep school. He used to often listen to western music on the European broadcasting service. I did not see it coming until one day I saw him carrying a guitar, which he told me was quite cheap and which he had asked his mother to get for him as a birthday present. I did not see any harm in this and thought it was a temporary hobby. I did not consider it necessary to make a big fuss as my parents once had done when they saw me playing the oud while sitting next to Hamida, the singer–belly dancer, for times have changed and the official educational policy has endorsed extracurricular school activities and young people's hobbies.

However, my son's hobby changed dramatically when he insisted to pursue and master it. His mother hired a professional Greek tutor who taught him how to play until he excelled at it. Later on I learned from his school principal that after he had been awarded his prep school certificate, he had formed a musical band at school that raised a lot of interest. With the advent of summer, he asked for my permission to join a band that would perform to a large audience during the vacation. I did not listen to him and absolutely refused permission. He acquiesced reluctantly. It was not until his last year in secondary school that he formed his present band, though on a small scale, and called it "Black Coats." During the summer vacation, he performed with it in public, unbeknown to me. He completed his secondary school education and joined the Film Institute. At this point, I was certain that music ran in his veins and that there was no hope of his abandoning it. It was then I realized there was no avoiding it. I read once that one of the great film directors had said that music with its rhythm is the right hand of any director. Therefore I kept silent and listened to him on the day he asked my permission to have a professor from the Conservatoire instruct him in the origins of harmony in music. Indeed this was beneficial for him in composing new pieces of music and redistributing old musical compositions in a new way especially for his band. I also allowed him to travel to Italy and other countries on musical tours. All this took place, according to him, as if he had wrested my permission from me. He felt that he had made his own way amid the mist of indifference between us. He only received encouragement and moral support from his mother. The only topic he and I talked about was his institute. He sometimes practiced at home and the loud sound of his instruments and melodies was met only with the closed door of my room.

Thus, as he would say, nothing had changed. There was still a gap between the generations. Yet this situation did not seem to bother him much; in fact, he may have found that it was better and more comfortable for him that I remain at a distance from his field.

But what he really desired—together with other sons—was to see his father share with him at least a few interests as he lives his age to the full. He is skilled in swimming, underwater fishing, and hunting with a rifle. He excels in archery, drives a car, loves to go on trips and adventures, and likes experimental films with their new waves and new fashions of dress. He is the son of his age. But when he looks around him he finds a different age. He finds a father of the classical type.

Is the gap between generations an inevitable one that cannot be altered? Or is it possible to correct this situation through understanding and cooperation? We are now in an age where a fierce collision between the young generation and the previous one is taking place on an unprecedented scale. The crux of the matter is that every previous generation believed that it alone could pass the correct judgment on the affairs of the age and that on it alone could fall the responsibility of shaping the present and forming the future, considering itself more experienced as having passed through the various stages of life. Young people used to accept this belief with respect and without any discussion until wars, disasters, and famines opened the gates of hell on earth in a most horrific way. The young were the firewood and fuel. They realized that all this had taken place under the directions of the older generation. They began to wonder, "How can the older generation call themselves experienced?"

The elderly have not learned from their mistakes throughout history. Doubt began to spread in young people's minds. The strongholds of the elderly began to shake. Confidence in them collapsed.

But young people have not formed their own strongholds yet, being new to their revolution and their own sense of self. They do not yet have clear organized ideas. It is like the onset of any revolution when the old strongholds are destroyed and it stands at a loss for some time not knowing what to do next. Thus when the revolt of youth broke out in France and shook De Gaulle's regime, there was no clear philosophy behind it. Only one or two young people were able to give voice to it. Their ideas were neither convincing nor well thought out. When they wanted slogans, there were conflicting trends. Ultimately they ended up holding pictures of exemplary honorable freedom fighters such as Guevara, Ho Chi Minh, and Mao

Tse-tung. Thus the sons of millionaires and poor commoners were placed on equal footing.

Governments were at a loss in the face of this revolt, for it is more dangerous to them than workers' strikes and farmers' demands: the rebellions of sectors are based on specific demands such as raising wages or improving living standards. However, the cries of young people all over the world cannot be easily defined. It is the cry of the whole age. It is the awakening of an alarming future. The future is no longer a vague word. It is an active moving machine that stands on two feet before us in the image of young people who will live in the year 2000 and beyond. They will find themselves standing alone when all those who belong to the old generation have disappeared. The young do not want to reach the threshold of the next century being pushed from behind by the minds that caused the world to decay through the politics of the previous century. But how is that to be achieved?

What can be done if young people have lost trust, and at the same time do not know what to do? Here lies the confusion that appears in their unusual behavior. The more they rebel, the more the previous generation entrench themselves in their strongholds and the dividing gap between the generations becomes wider. Since trust is lost, the old words too have become subject to doubt. Advice, guidance, admonition, and other words the old generations use have become, in young people's view, a source of ridicule synonymous with domination and arrogance regardless of the desire for benefit and the intention of reform.

My son used to remain politely silent whenever I advised or admonished him in matters of concern to him. But as soon as he left me, he would whisper to others, "He wants to exercise his parental authority!" So our means of communication with the young generation must change and we must alter the way we address them. We must search for a new type of language and a new way to reach an understanding with them. First and foremost, we should avoid addressing them from behind the walls of our old strongholds. We have to leave our world and go to theirs. The idea that the stages of life are connected like the rungs of a ladder that lead to a top rung that oversees and dominates the rest of the rungs is an idea that is no longer acceptable today. What is acceptable today is that every stage has its own character, individuality, laws, language, and concepts, in other words, its own world. The different stages of life are not rungs in a ladder but rather carriages of a train. Every carriage is different and separate from the other, carrying different passengers and different freights. Yet they are connected by a narrow door, and the whole train heads to its inevitable destination. The middle-aged and the elderly passengers of the last carriage cannot possibly understand or know what goes on in the young people's carriage unless they go and sit among them. That is no easy matter, for the movement of a passenger from one carriage to another makes people regard him with some trepidation. Silence will descend upon the passengers and they will not feel at ease or talk until they feel reassured. This will not happen unless he is able to gain their trust, understand their worries, and speak their language. Success in this is not always certain. There are thinkers like Marcuse[1] who wanted to defend the youth and spoke their language, but some of them applauded merely because a prominent thinker was on their side. The lawyer who stands by his client and wins the

1. Herbert Marcuse (1898–1979) was a German philosopher and sociologist who immigrated to the United States in 1933. He taught philosophy and politics at Columbia and Harvard Universities. Marcuse was concerned with student movements in the 1960s in the United States.

case is not necessarily the one who will win his heart and live in his mind.

There lies the difficulty for whoever thinks of embarking on a journey to the world of the new generation. It is more difficult for someone like me who does not have the common ground of contemporary interests or a free spirit. Thus when my friends at *Al-Ahram*[2] newspaper encouraged me to go and see my son and his band, the suggestion took me aback, for I found it not only difficult but also impossible to accept. Nowadays I do not go out at night, let alone stay up till after midnight! They tried to make this more appealing and easier for me to accept by saying that spending one night out was a small price to pay to understand these young people. They also said it was strange for a witness of the age to lose the sense of curiosity to such an extent.

I told them to wait till I asked my son first, to see how this idea would affect him. Would he really be pleased if I went or would he be apprehensive? When I raised the subject with him, he listened carefully then raised his head and said in a doubtful tone that he knew already my feelings about them and what I would say. He told me that when Frank Sinatra heard his daughter singing—she was a professional singer like him—and was asked his opinion, he belittled her performance and accused her of being ignorant of the basic rules of the profession. Charlie Chaplin did the same when his children became professional actors. It is an old well-known act for a great artist to depreciate his children either out of a sense of superiority or for the sake of appearances or for fear of being accused of bias or flattery.

2. *Al-Ahram* is a national newspaper in Egypt to which many leading writers contribute.

I reassured him that this would not happen. Maybe if his profession were similar to mine, that is, literature and writing, I would have showered him with criticism and exhausted him with my observations. I would have also been unable to stop myself from reacting in the same way as Sinatra and Chaplin, both of whom share the same profession with their children. However, we have different professions so my son should not worry. Moreover, I would not permit myself to delve into a subject I was ignorant of. I would be just like any ordinary member of the audience. I promised him that I would remove from my soul any preconceived ideas and from my mind any personal point of view. Furthermore, I would not look upon the band with an arrogant, deprecatory, or challenging attitude.

Regardless of my preferences in art, I would hate to be somebody who would belittle other people's preferences. I also do not intend to be the thinker who would safeguard in towers his taste in types of art that have been sanctified for centuries, and who looks down upon other new types that are still regarded with suspicion without having the courage to try to appreciate them or risk talking about them. I confess that I was and perhaps still am this type of person, for I have written scornfully of jazz. I remember that when Jean-Paul Sartre and Simone de Beauvoir came to Egypt, I criticized this type of music but to my surprise both thinkers spoke highly of jazz, confirming what they had already published in books, particularly in Sartre's *Situations* (1947). It was then that I realized that they did not want to distance themselves from trying to appreciate and understand whatever was connected to the spirit of the age.

But the question now is, what is the spirit of the age? The answer is not simple, and it is my opinion that we should sense it in the most obvious signs. Undoubtedly the most obvious characteristics that distinguish the spirit of the age are its quick tempo and its resounding commotion. This is because in our modern age in the span of a year, events occur and discoveries and adventures are made that used to happen over the course of a hundred years. It is no longer the age for sitting down contemplating but is of dynamic thought. This is reflected in the young people who opened their eyes to find themselves in the heart of the new age and could not bear to remain inactive or quiet. They want to move with this dynamic age to its stirring, resounding music. They do not want to sit languidly pinned to a chair with eyes half closed, listening to a reflective type of music. They want not merely to listen but also to participate. They do not want to remain in one place but aspire to go everywhere, to explore the world on foot, jump into a passing car, and sprawl on the deck of a passing ship unhampered by lack of money, fear of danger or the unknown.

One of the most important characteristics of young people nowadays is that they have discerned by innate instinct the greatest vision of the future, which is "world unity." Just as the astronaut in outer space perceives the planet earth from without as one united entity, so do young people on earth see it from within. They are all united—the white, the black, and the yellow—in many of their tastes, objectives, and human ideals. They have come together everywhere in almost the same costume and dance to express the contemporary movement and herald a united future. It is therefore an indication and a sign. Perhaps it is not a passing wave, for it may be that the age dyes the youth with its own colors and makes them move to its own rhythm. On top of that, when I was in Paris in the late seventies, I saw the spread of barbers' shops where women gave men a haircut. The shops bore a sign bearing the word "Unisex" where there is no difference between a man's and a woman's haircut. Dr. Hussein Fawzy and I saw a production of Shakespeare's play *King Lear* performed by a group called

"La Jeunesse" (Youth) in a modernist style that they term "the shock method." The audience was shocked to find old King Lear portrayed as a young man who is dynamic and violent, chasing his daughters, kicking them and screeching Shakespeare's verse. We both prayed to God to help this age, that of nuclear bombs, Picasso's paintings, and unisex! Will this mad age last for another century? I do not think so.

The last century was one of seated contemplation, but the present is the century of "insane" swift thinking. After the middle of the last century, the initial desire for movement represented in Johann Strauss's waltzes was received with enthusiasm by the people in pubs and byways. The melody of "The Blue Danube" knocked at the gates of palaces to the horror of the nobility, aristocrats, religious people, and judicious thinkers who considered it scandalous. Yet classical music continued to evolve until some theories appeared that regarded discordance as a form of innovation.

It was not a temporary wave as traditionalists always expect but an answer to the cry of the nuclear age, the signs of which have undoubtedly begun to appear. These signs continued to develop into styles and transformations that changed the waltz from its past form into other forms represented in the current forms of dance music. The waltz, which was regarded in its age as full of movement, is now regarded as the epitome of sedateness.

But what are we elderly people doing, who lived long in the glories of the past century and became used to reflective music and whose bodies do not respond to lively music?

There is no doubt that our old music will continue to survive, for humanity will always be in need of its beautiful lasting heritage. But the problem is, should we lock ourselves up with our surviving treasures and close our ears to the noise our sons make? Or should we open our ears and try to understand what they are doing? More importantly, should we try very hard to appreciate the things they appreciate, until we meet them even halfway?

This would be my endeavor, and I decided to proceed with God's help. Fearing last-minute hesitation on my part, the artist Salah Taher insisted on accompanying me in his capacity as Ismail's professor at the Film Institute, saying that he was the best person to understand my son's artistic nature. Dr. Youssef Idris wished to join us, being closer to young people than either of us and the most interested in studying them. He was also most astonished at my lack of knowledge of my son's performances, which he had long wished that I should attend.

But why wasn't anyone just as surprised that my son does not attend the performances of my plays? My son was asked once about this and he said, "It is fortunate that I do not write literature and he does not play music, that he remains in his field and I remain in mine and that neither of us interferes in the other's business."

This reminded me of an old story that happened between my father and me that shows that sons find their fathers' interference in their affairs irritating. It was on a day in 1935, when I was the director of investigations in the Ministry of Education as well as a well-known writer, that my father paid me a visit in my office. A reporter was interviewing me concerning literature and art. I was taken aback when my father interfered in the interview, wanting to direct it the way he pleased, correcting my opinions in keeping with his own views and beliefs. I felt that I was brushed aside and treated as if I were still a child.

This same feeling is felt by my son today when I interfere in his affairs. He repeats the same words: "My father still sees me as a child!" It seems that nothing is more psychologically detrimental than this idea.

I remember another incident involving my father when a copy of the manuscript of my play *Scheherazade* (1934) accidentally fell into his hands before it was published. He read in it a phrase describing Scheherazade's beautiful body and the lust lurking in the darkness. He came to me and said with disgust, "What is this shameful talk that violates the rules of decency. This is rudeness; you must immediately remove these indecent phrases." Later I said to myself, "What if he had lived to read 'The Red Notebook,'[3] a chapter in my novel *The Sacred Bond* (1944)!"

ᔓ

The time had come to see Ismail and his band. How many years had passed since I set foot in a dance hall? Would I be able to tolerate the dancing and dancers? I recalled the days of my youth in the early twenties. The day we first landed in Paris, two of my lifelong friends, the late Dr. Helmy Bahgat Badawi and Dr. Mustafa El Kolaly, tempted me to take dance lessons with them. They stressed the importance of dancing in that country and the necessity of mastering it for those who hoped to be invited to parties and mingle with society. Therefore I succumbed to their wishes. A helpful person introduced us to a dance instructor called Arturo who asked each of us for the equivalent of one Egyptian pound and gave each a small notepad containing ten tickets, each ticket entitling one to a lesson. He assured us that after ten lessons we would be skillful dancers. So we went to our first lesson. He began with my two friends. No sooner had he begun to take steps and circle with

3. In al-Hakim's novel *The Sacred Bond*, the heroine is an adulterous wife who confesses her relationship with an actor, describing all the minute details and her feelings. This type of relationship was and still is a grave social and religious taboo in Egyptian society.

them than the signs of skill and success appeared. But as for me, in spite of the sedateness of the dances of those times, after the first step and spin I felt that the world had turned black and that my head was whirling with dizziness. I quickly divided my tickets between my friends and was content with the visit as the only booty gained.

Therefore, may God make this night an easy one for such as me, and may it end well! Finally, my companions bore me to the car. And soon I found myself in the midst of dim lights and suddenly bright colorful ones that dazzled my eyes. The dancing was in full swing on the floor, brightly shining eyes were drawn to it, heads and souls seemed to me to be swaying over plentifully laden tables, and food and drink were going to and fro on dishes that seemed to be flying around me in the air. I was like a rustic in a *Moulid,*[4] his first ever. My astonishment was no doubt expected by the two conspirators from *Al-Ahram*. I was astounded, and for a few moments I did not know where my feet were or where they were taking me. I let my companions lead the way and seat me wherever they wished. I cannot and do not want to describe that night. I had made my companions promise not to stay too long after midnight or else I would leave them. They promised to do so. We began to look around us, to become absorbed, and gradually adapt to our surroundings. They then surprised me by informing me that it was almost three o'clock in the morning. I jumped off my chair, shouting, "How did this happen?"

4. *Moulid* means birthday in Arabic. It is a celebration of a holy person whether by Muslims or Christians in Egypt to honor their saints. The *Moulid* is a great festival where thousands of people celebrate by listening to Sufis and sheiks performing "zikr" (ritual dance). The festival also includes games, entertainment, and food. Candy is also sold here.

To tell the truth, I did not feel time passing nor did I feel bored. The exuberant liveliness of the young people around me was contagious. Sometimes health and sickness are equally contagious. I no longer doubted the fact that an old tree trunk entrenched in the earth can be affected by some of the pulsing vigor of the branches. For these branches that gently sway with the breeze and violently move with the wind, the law of their life is this motion we call dance. For centuries, there has been no force on earth that could stop this law. It had seemed to me that the trunk would be uprooted by the violent shaking of the branches and that it was afraid of this occurring. But who knows? Maybe this would please and delight it. Maybe it would see this as a sign of life for itself too, since it was as rigid as a piece of wood awaiting the woodworm. Moreover, the living trunk may benefit also by discovering the direction of the wind from the movement of the branches.

My companions drew my attention to Ismail holding his guitar and hugging his saxophone and moving from one to the other, playing on the one or blowing on the other. I did not see in him the quiet and silent son I always used to see at home who spoke very little about himself and his work. I sometimes encouraged him to talk and introduce topics he liked, such as well-known jazz virtuosos whose names I came across in foreign newspapers. It surprised me that jazz had become important enough to the extent that respected literary and artistic journals I read assigned it a regular column just like that assigned to classical music.

This topic would bring him a little out of his shell, for he is not the talkative type. Silence and brevity are more dominant in him than verbosity and elaboration. He knows and feels more than he says. From the little that he said, I gathered that he was very well read and informed about the art he had chosen. I also discovered that he is familiar with the classical music that I appreciate, and that he has his own views, especially his appreciation of Chopin's art and Beethoven's "Quartet," which I had neglected to give their proper due. He also believes that true jazz should be based on the principles of classical music, and then be free to add to it. This reassured me a little. I have always believed that the type of work does not matter and that the value of any work lies in delving into and perfecting it. Sometimes a big job could be belittled by the superficiality of people involved in it, while a simple job could be elevated by the seriousness of those involved. A speck of dust remains a speck of dust to those who see it as such, while it becomes a whole world of revolving celestial bodies to those who discover this in it.

During the interval, my companions suggested that we ask the members of the band to join us. The main objective was, like that of the "conspirators" from *Al-Ahram*, to bring together father and son and encourage the father to greet his son and write about the incident with his pen. It was a sensitive situation. Although it was natural for a father to greet his son, writing about it was extremely embarrassing. For a father like me, the feeling of anxiety is greater than that of satisfaction. I did not know how to satisfy the parties that pushed me into this situation. It seemed to me there was no way out except through honesty. I would be true to my feelings; that was enough. My feelings as a father are understandable. I do not want to dwell on them. But what was new was that I felt overwhelming joy, love, and sympathy for the young people in this band as a group uniquely connected by affection, friendship, and art. They instilled in me the happiness of youth. These cheerful, kind, and hardworking young people: I used to pass by them from a distance like a frightening ghost whom they dreaded as they were conducting their arduous rehearsals patiently, tirelessly, and persistently. I used to avoid them for fear of embarrassing them or making them feel I was interfering in their work. There was a wall between us. That night was the first time for us to meet and shake hands, and I felt that they too were happy with this encounter.

The most important outcome of that night, from my point of view, was that this encounter with the young people made me feel that it was possible to remove the walls between the generations.

14

The Responsibilities of Young Writers of Literature

We are on the threshold, today, of a new phase in modern Arabic literature when young writers are about to receive the torch that will light the future. It is a responsibility the weight of which they undoubtedly have began to feel on their shoulders. Therefore they have discussed new problems concerning which they considered it their duty to express a firm opinion. Thus they have argued about classical and colloquial Arabic, literature, art for art's sake, and many more topics that, once opened, lead to endless debate.

There is no objection to the discussion of such topics, nor is there harm in having conflicting viewpoints in the fields of literature, art, and thought. All these discussions will be in vain, God willing, in the true artist's conscience. For a true artist is not influenced by mere talk and is devoted to his work. No opinion in literature and art is of value by itself, and it will not live unless it has an effect.

In literature and art, you must first create an effect that conveys your thoughts to the generations. Therefore all these discussions and opinions—as long as they fly in the air and are not accompanied by work—will not be of any value to people nor will they last. A valuable work is everything in literature and art; creative craftsmanship alone is what remains deeply rooted as it is imbued with the spirit of lasting life.

The question here that arises is, what is a valuable work? Is it the one written in classical or in colloquial Arabic? Is it the one that addresses a special group or the one written for the general public? Is literature for life's sake or is art for art's sake? If we look for an answer in great world literatures, we will find that each one of their schools has its acknowledged value and lasting effect.

A valuable work is a valuable work; that is all. Nevertheless, we should try to define the meaning of "value" in an artistic work. Though it is a difficult task, I shall try anyway. I believe the value of a work of art lies in its form: its perfection, mastery, excellence, and competence. Even when a writer resorts to colloquial language, he should do so not out of lack of competence or avoidance of formal language but because of excellence, competence, and the artistic desire to achieve precision of expression. This was done by Robert Louis Stevenson, one of the finest British poets to write in a formal style, when he let the sailors converse in their rather obscure colloquial dialect. This was also done by Charles Dickens and Georges Courteline.

Competence, mastery, proficiency, and the aspiration for perfection are the attributes of valuable works with regard to style and form. As for content, the most prominent attributes are humanity: whatever affects human beings in every time and place, whatever makes a human being more refined, and whatever leads his society to a better destiny. All of this should be in the framework of lasting, refined, and wonderful artistic and literary pleasure.

In my point of view, proficiency, entertainment, and humanity are the most important qualities in works of literature and art.

Whoever produces a work of literature or art that is not proficient in artistic style or precise literary expression, have they failed in matters of form?

Whoever produces a work that is neither delightful nor impressive has produced something other than literature or art.

Whoever produces a delightful, entertaining, proficient work that is devoid of human significance and motivating ideas for human beings and society would have made a literary or artistic work that is skillfully made but of little value, like a piece of cheap shining glass not a precious stone.

Now let us return to the responsibility of young writers of literature, or those who are so called nowadays, those on whose efforts the literary and artistic movements will be based in the next twenty or thirty years. What is the true nature of the responsibility cast on their backs?

First of all, they should be guardians of true values in thought and art and innovate as much as they want but within the framework of proficiency, excellence, and perfection. To this end, they should combat the spirit of frivolity, carelessness, and vulgarity in anything that touches upon literature and art. This fast-moving era with its press and radio, the age of public education for the wide masses who consume cheap literary and artistic merchandise, ultimately destroys true literature that originates from real talent if the young writers, the leaders of the future, do not strongly protect good works. They should act as a protective dam that will prevent the infiltration of rotten mental consummation into the souls of the people. It is also their duty to protect the freedom and responsibility of literature. In my view, the free writer is the only one conscientiously responsible for what he writes and produces as a service to mankind and the society as he alone sees fit. For the true free writer of literature is the one responsible in his own eyes.

Young writers of literature are responsible for their new society in their own eyes and those of literary history because they will directly influence it through their writings in the next twenty or thirty years. Their impact will be the model and the example for the new generation of youth and teenagers today.

Somebody may ask, "What will be the impact of our generation in the next twenty or thirty years?" I say, "Who knows? Maybe our books will be read tomorrow as we read today the books Al Muwaylihi and El Manfaloti.[1] Our styles may become suitable for historical study but not suitable for contemporary use."

Can today's author write in the style of Al Muwaylihi or Hefni Nasif[2] style without being ridiculed?

Does anybody in England today write in the style of Shakespeare or even Thackeray, or with the art of Thomas Hardy or Galsworthy?

A literary issue arises here. What then is the real impact of the ancients? What is the value of the art of past generations to the rising generations?

To answer such a question, we must differentiate between imitation and guidance, and between approach and formation.

1. Mohamed Al Muwaylihi (1868–1930) was an Egyptian writer and journalist. One of his well-known works is *Hadith Isa Ibn Hisham* (*The Story of Isa Ibn Hisham*), which criticized the social conditions in Egypt under British rule. His works contributed to the rise of modern Arabic literature. His style is not accessible to laymen, being rather poetic and full of rhetoric. Mostafa El Manfaloti (1876–1924) was an Egyptian writer and poet. He was one of the pioneers in the first movement of the Egyptian literary revival in the modern age. He was also one of the leaders of social reform who held the banner of civilization and intellectual enlightenment for the whole nation.

2. Hefni Nasif (1860–1919) was an Egyptian writer and poet.

The fact is that the new generation only imitates the contemporary writers closest to them as they are directly in contact with their new styles of writing. But no one can rightly be called a writer of literature or an artist unless he absorbs the art of the old generations and is guided by them in his artistic and literary formation.

Literary and artistic styles are continuously evolving. But the styles of the past generations must all contribute to the formation of the new literary writer or modern artist.

To sum up, our literature in the next twenty or thirty years may make our generation eligible for the task of guidance and formation, but it will hand the actual leadership and direct models to the young writers. With these examples before them, they will give the literary scene a new color.

This is their responsibility . . . What a great responsibility!

15

Young People and Innovation in Poetry

I am not one of those people who cling to the pillars of ancient poetry with their meters and rhyme schemes without argument or discussion, for I am always ready to listen to every new opinion. Not all poetry that is written in the old styles do I like. Among contemporary poets, there are some who try to imitate the old styles by using grand preambles, abstruse and well-composed diction, a resonating meter, and a strict rhyme. Thus I find the versifier but not the poet. Nowadays there are those among us who claim that they are great poets merely because they own an Arabic dictionary, are adept in rhyme and meter, and find those who believe them and think that they write poetry.

No true poet presents a rock without filling it with life. No true poet scoops commonplace words from the river of prose.

That is as far as "form" is concerned. If we leave form and focus on content, it will require another study. What are the new meanings that the new poetry must deal with? I use the word "must" unwillingly, as I am against any coercion in art in general and in poetry in particular. But the word "must" is in common use today among young poets and writers and their critics, so there is no harm if it is used in this context.

Is any subject dealt with in newspapers and discussed in public gatherings suitable for poetry? Can subjects for prose also be suitable for poetry?

It may be said that poetry is an art of suggestion and not of information. It is like the lantern of Aladdin that reveals to you the hidden treasures deep within you. It is not a full sack that you can empty into your vacant safes.

That is why the subject that poetry deals with should be suited to the nature of its message. The subject therefore should be clear, illuminating, and refined so that it could have the power of discovery and suggestion. It should not be a dull subject in the media that would fill one's head with limited material. It should not be repeated news, interviews, dates, or incidents that prose has already overconsumed, the only remaining possibility for poetry being to put it in "cans" of "preserved" verse forms.

All this may be said and all this is on the whole correct. But in art, I always prefer to rely on the artist more than on the word "must." To me, the artist is a magician who should not be asked what he has done, for as long as he is a true and genuine artist he is able to do anything with his miraculous magic. He is capable, with his talent, of raising an ordinary subject to the most sublime level of poetry, whereas the base, fraudulent artist can bring down the poetic subject to the level of vulgarity or mere information.

One deduces from all these points that true innovation in Arabic poetry in form and content will not be genuine or serious unless it is built on a tremendous reservoir of culture, talent, and experience that can challenge, combat, and overcome the difficulties. There is no art nowadays that requires greater efforts to elevate it than that of poetry. This applies not just to Arabic poetry but to poetry in every language. It has even been said that our age is not the age of poetry because of the extent of dislike and indifference that it meets everywhere. Today there are few publishing firms in the civilized capitals of the world that would be willing to publish an anthology of poems, and few theatrical companies—with rare exceptions—that would risk directing a verse play. The great poet who can impose his genius on his age is not to be found in the world nowadays with the power and magnificence that he had in previous centuries. All that are found today are obscure or desperate attempts at innovation in poetry on a narrow scale by enthusiastic intellectuals. Does this mean that the age of democracy and popular culture is the age of prose? Or does it mean that this modern age has not yet succeeded in finding the poetic style that suits and represents it?

It is a question that so far remains without an answer. There is no answer to such questions until the actual appearance of a poet who represents the age and produces true innovations.

When will he appear? How will he appear? No one knows. This age is in real need of him. When he appears, he will bring with him his new style, which befits his age.

16

A Warning to the New Poetry of the Young

Some may think that if you wish to be a new poet, all you need to do is find a topic that is covered in daily newspapers and written in prose, and divide it into sentences of varied length. Then put each sentence in a line, and it does not matter if the line sometimes consists of one or two words. It is preferable if between one line and the next there is a line or two of rhymed prose, so that it would strike the ear as narration or a melody.

No, this is nothing but fake new poetry, not true poetry. Personally, I rarely like the New Poetry but I find those who write it real innovators even if they break with all the old restrictions. This is because they are poets, gifted ones in spite of everything.

But I would like to sound a warning. The ease with which it appears to be written occasionally tempts everyone to be a poet. I did not realize this danger until some people admitted that the objective of this new method is to be free of the restrictions of meter and rhyme that were imposed by classical poetry. In other words, they wanted to avoid the difficulties by eliminating them. Eliminating difficulties is always admirable except in art, because art is difficult and should always be difficult in order to be art. The artist is the person to confront difficulty and transform it into simplicity; that is his miracle. It is said that art is magic or a type of magic; it was so in early times when it was practiced by magicians and priests. Its impact on people was derived from the belief that it was something miraculous that could not be practiced by everyone, but became pliable and easy in the hands of a priest or magician or an artist.

Therefore, the first condition is for art to be difficult to attain until the artist comes and subjects it to his abilities and talent, and palatable and easy for people to appreciate. Art is a solid rock from which the artist should extract cool water. Art is not a flowing river from which the wayfarer can drink effortlessly. Art must therefore involve difficulties, obstacles, and restrictions and succeeds by overcoming them, not by doing away with them. The skilled player is the one who wins by abiding by the rules of the game. If he abolishes or simplifies its rules, what would be the value of winning?

I can understand that rules or restrictions are abolished because they are absurd, but not because they are difficult. In this case, new conditions must be set for the new art such as musicality, imagery, and a driving, motivating force without need for a rhyme after that. However, to abolish rules for the sake of making it easy for the artist is a principle dangerous to the existence of art itself. It is true that the new art seems to be easy, but it is not at all easy. It seems easy from the point of view of people but not from the point of view of the artist. It is that which the artist toils, suffers, and struggles to create and present to the public in order to make it delightful and easy for them to comprehend to the extent that they think they could do the same without any labor or strain.

That is what they call magic in art. It is what causes people to think it is within their reach, but in reality it is more remote than the stars. Great art is this: what seems easy for people but is difficult for the artist.

17

Honesty Is the Basis for Young People's Innovation

One day some young literary writers were alarmed by a critical movement launched by other young writers, which they described as "intimidation." The latter suddenly filled newspapers and books with studies stuffed with words such as "literature for life," "flowery literature," "bourgeois literature," passivism, positivism, form and content, the organic, nonorganic, and many other terms. Then with the appearance of the translation of some literary publications and journals published in Eastern European and Asian countries, the secret was revealed and the source of these words became clear. The first group of young people was thus reassured and started to relax and breathe easily, while the second group was ashamed and the battle almost abated.

The reason why the first group was reassured was that they had previously believed that such literary judgments were truly made according to natural criteria whose origin and natural source were undoubtedly found in our land. When they realized that these were imported criteria that were the subject of controversy in other countries, these studies began to seem less valuable in their eyes.

The reason why the second group was ashamed was that they were hiding—very skillfully—the source of their criteria and terminology to make people assume that it was their own personal effort. They gave the impression that these were the ultimate natural criteria on which the literature and art of our country must be based today as well as yesterday, and should even be applied to all literature and art which appeared on earth in any time or place without argument or debate. When the facts were revealed and it became clear that all these terms and criteria were translated and copied from other literatures and expressed the views of other peoples and countries where they sprang naturally, that group of critics felt that their position has been unfavorably defined. They felt that literary writers had begun to regard them as merely promoters of a movement, no more and no less. This is approximately the final result of a literary battle that has occupied the minds of young people in recent years.

It is regrettable that the battle has ended or abated in this way, as we need something to revitalize the field of literary and artistic thought. I believe that this battle could have strongly and continually benefitted literature and art if it had been established from the start on a different basis. What is that basis?

First of all, it should be based on honesty. For any structure that is based on honesty will last in literature, art, and all else. All our previous literary and artistic movements were built on honesty and accordingly survived and became the foundation of our true cultural renaissance. Honesty in these movements means that they did not conceal anything or delude anyone but simply said, we are in need of Western thought to add what is not found in our heritage and we will transfer what we need for our literary and artistic renovation.

This process of transfer and translation was carried out in broad daylight as has occurred in every nation and age. All other literatures grew, flourished, and received new air, for every renovation in thought, like the renewal of air in a room, requires opening the windows.

In this way, previous movements avoided that sense of shame, embarrassment, and reaction that occurs when a hidden and frightful truth is exposed. No doubt this movement of the group of young people would have been respected and would have appeared to be serious and lasting if they had simply said, "We need to open the window on the east just as the window on the west was opened before," and if they had made an honest transfer and an accurate translation of the literary and critical classics from the eastern countries without distortion, fraudulence, or deception.

No rational person can deny this truth: renovating rooms and renaissances requires the opening of closed windows in all directions. Something similar happened in the days of the Islamic cultural renaissance during the age of Mammon when the movement of the transference and translation of great Persian, Indian, Greek, and Roman works thrived, as well as those of various other civilizations. It may be said that they did not possess such honesty at all times. That is true. And that is why they have an excuse.

However, the excuse does not relieve them of their responsibility for the outcome. We excuse them but we also excuse those who belittled them when their mask fell off.

That is the first point, as I have noted, but there is a second cause of a weak foundation and perhaps it is the quickest one for the loss of confidence, namely, faulty application. No sooner had this group of young people found some models in the literature, art, and literary studies of these eastern and other countries than they became filled with arrogance and began—thoughtlessly and hastily—to write and criticize, and the outcome in poetry, the short story, and research was a hasty product that was mainly artificial. They tried to apply the imported ideas to a different society from that which these ideas came from, and to a literature that is dissimilar to the literature of these other countries in its heritage, history, and stages of development.

All the above made that movement, which could have been truly a renovating one, lose some of its credibility. Instead of our intellectual, literary, and artistic renaissance being able to benefit from the advantages of the eastern window as it had benefitted before from the advantages of the western one, the matter almost turned into a farce, and trust started to crumble. Ironic or doubtful smiles were the response to hands stretched out to many of these publications that appear today in poetry, the short story, or criticism written by some of these advocates calling for this type of renovation from the young writers of literature.

Thus this group has unwittingly damaged their movement. If only that were the end of the matter! For if it was interpreted as faulty application, the damage would be limited to its narrow confines. But since the mask has fallen, the group is regarded by intellectuals as representing or being influenced by these Eastern literatures. But why should these literatures, which are mostly of the highest standards, also be dragged through the dust clouds of ridicule and loss of confidence?

What can save the situation now? I believe the only solution is to attempt a true movement of renovation, which calls for respect and is based on hard, slow labor, great patience, and deep study. We should study our society seriously. We should study our literature and art objectively and meticulously, encompassing their stages of development connected with the development of the society. Our new and evolving literature should be the natural outcome of social and intellectual development. Our guiding light in all of the above should be honesty, open-mindedness, and proper application.

18

Young People and the Devil

The dialogue I am about to recount took place one winter night at midnight, that terrifying hour when all myths agree that something momentous usually happens. I was sitting at my desk reading under a faint light, with piles of books stacked in front of me covered with dust. The book open in my hands was *Faust.* I had reached the part where the old scientist was sitting one night among his books, his white hair hanging over his shoulders, despairing of learning and disinterested in life that did not grant him the knowledge he thought it could grant to human beings. He sat there counting the eighty years which he had lived. What had he accomplished in them? What had he gained? He had never felt what it was like to be young and the joy of life had never filled his heart. His soul had never known the meaning of peace and a smile even at that lovely time when his peers were speaking of "love" while he was speaking of "knowledge."

He had really worked hard to achieve knowledge. He had tried to grasp everything a human mind could grasp. He had devoted all his life to learning, and now that this life was about to end, now that he was on his way back to that unknown place he had come from—if we could call it a place—don't you think he was going back to it empty-handed?

Knowledge itself is now mocking him just as he is mocking himself; he has lost a whole life for its sake, one in which there are many things other than knowledge. He is leaving life without ever having held a flower or smelled the scent of the magnificent orchard with its trees, rivers, flowers, and deer. He never filled his heart with anything but filled his head with many words that will be eaten by worms, as Hayne[1] once said, with whatever flesh will be eaten from this large skull!

All these musings were circling in the mind of Faust the scientist as he sat reading a book on astrology in dim light in a room of the Middle Ages. There was nothing around him but piles of books covered with dust and total terrifying silence, and no one was there.

Yet a shiver passed through the scientist's old body, as he felt he was not alone in the room. He hesitated a little, then searched the corners of the room with his dim eyes but did not find anything but the shadows of the lighted lantern that were chasing each other on the wall like playful ghosts. He was stricken with a fear he could not account for. He turned his face to his book and tried to continue reading to feel peace of mind.

Suddenly a voice whispered in his ears, "Faust! Faust! I heard what you were thinking!"

The blood froze in the old man's veins.

The voice continued, "Don't be afraid! Don't you know who I am?" The scientist was unable to answer, did not dare to move and sat there like a waxwork statue.

The voice resumed: "I am the one who can grant you what you want."

At this point, the old man was filled with power and his fear vanished. He turned in the direction of the voice and saw

1. Paul Hamilton Hayne (1830–1886) was a nineteenth-century American poet, critic, and editor.

an unusual face that did not resemble a human face, smiling a strange smile. He could not find a body to that face as it was enveloped in darkness. The old man tried to pull himself together and said in a trembling voice, "Who are you?"

The face looked at him again and replied, "Does it really matter to you to know who I am?"

"Who are you?"

"You always want to know. Always the love of knowledge! You mortal fool! Isn't it enough that I will give you what you want? All you want."

"Who are you?"

"The Devil."

The scientist was astounded and looked at the face again, and found it smiling that unchanging smile. He slowly repeated and whispered as if to himself, "The Devil."

The face moved a little closer to the old man and said in a pleasant tone, "Are you afraid of me? Don't be afraid. Wait."

At once the old man saw two arms, two feet, and the rest of a human body come flying obediently from the different parts of the room, attaching themselves to the face until it appeared as a human being. The face changed and became like a human face. The man stretched his hand out to a chair next to the old man and sat down, saying as if to himself, "Here I am a human being like you. I have to be a human being like you so that you can understand me. O human being! You cannot see except someone in your own image. I am at your service!"

The scientist's fear subsided a little and he remembered how a moment ago he had been upset and dissatisfied with his life, so he shifted in his seat and cried, "O Devil! Give me . . . Give me . . ."

"Ask for whatever you want!"

"Youth." The old man said it from the bottom of his weak heart.

The Devil answered calmly, "Granted. But what will you give me in exchange? The devil does not give anything for nothing!"

The old man answered immediately, "I will give you knowledge. All the knowledge I have acquired over the past eighty years."

The Devil laughed out loud, saying, "I have no need for this commodity. Your knowledge is of no use to me. I need something else from you."

"What?"

"Your soul."

The old man did not hesitate. "It is yours."

The Devil quickly stretched out his hand in the air, picked up a sheet of paper, and opened it under the lamp. He then caught the old man's arm, startling him.

"What are you doing?"

"Don't be afraid of anything. I want a little of your blood so you can write a contract on this sheet of paper. It is a pledge between us: I give you youth and you give me your soul!"

The old man complied and wrote the pact with his own blood. The Devil picked up the written contract, raised his hand in the air, then placed it on the old man's body. His old age suddenly fell away from him as withered leaves fall from a young tree. The old scientist suddenly turned into a young man of twenty years of age, handsome in appearance, with a smiling countenance, a spirit full of joy, and a heart that yearned for love.

No sooner had I finished reading this scene in *Faust* than I cast the book aside and began to ponder in the valley of contemplation. What really possessed me at that time was the love of "knowledge." My dreams were to open a window every morning, overlooking an unknown world of the worlds of this universe that is floating in seas of secrets. Whoever revealed to my eager eyes something new was worthy of being given anything from me that he wished. That night I shouted in the room, "Devil! Devil! Show yourself to me; take from me whatever you wish, and give me what I want!"

Nobody appeared, of course. The walls did not split open and the shout I uttered was nothing but a sound reverberating inside me. In reality, it was just a whisper that did not reach the door of the room. Presently I fell into a partial slumber in which a stage was erected in my imagination and there stood the Devil wearing Mephistopheles' red clothes, his hands on the hilt of his sword, a cunning cynical smile on his lips, looking at me and saying, "Did you summon me?"

I whispered, "Yes!"

"What do you want from me?"

"Knowledge."

He gave a long, loud laugh, which made the feather on his horn flutter, and said, "Are you aware of the scope of this word?"

I understood what he meant, so I shouted, "Yes! Yes! I know that you too do not know the scope of this word. I did not want the impossible from you. I did not mean that you give me 'knowledge' itself, but I wanted you to grant me the 'love of knowledge.' I want you to grant me the kind of soul that lives for knowledge. I want you to give me what you took from Faust! Give me Faust's soul that you took from him. I want to have the soul of Faust or the soul of Goethe!"

"What would you give me in exchange?"

"Anything you want."

"Youth."

"It is yours!"

I said it without hesitation, and Mephistopheles gave me a long look. A look of wonder and pity—if the devil could sometimes feel pity—or the look of a wily merchant in a losing deal made by a gullible minor, and said, "You'll regret it."

"Never!"

"I can understand that people would pay a high price to have 'youth' but to see a young man pay . . . listen to my advice, young man. I am not used to giving sincere advice to anyone, but let me tell you: nothing in the world can compensate for youth!"

"Knowledge . . . knowledge . . . knowledge."

The Devil gave a short cynical laugh and said as if he was speaking to himself, "Faust used to say that when he was young!"

I said with blind enthusiasm, "The love of knowledge is the youth of the mind. It is eternal youth. It represents human exaltedness to which the angels prostrated themselves except for you, O insolent one on the throne of our enlightened thought!"

"The throne of your enlightened thought? What shall I say to this young man?"

"I know you and I abhor you. You're here on this earth with one sole objective, which is to extinguish the light in these great lamps that ornament our bodies. You hold a long stick like the ones that were carried by 'night demons' with which they extinguished gas lamps in the alleyways at the break of dawn!"

"How absurd gas lamps are!"

"Yes, but they are no longer in use because of electricity! Night demons with their sticks disappeared with them. It is time that you too should disappear with your sword and feather as no one will sell his 'lamp' today for anything."

"Faust sold his lamp for a girl."

"It was a gas lamp."

"Whether gas or electricity, light is always light."

"O enemy of light! Give me light and take from me whatever you wish."

The Devil said, "I will."

He took off his cap and bowed to me in an exaggerated manner, his cap touching the floor, just like Alexander Dumas's knights. He turned to leave but I stopped him and said, "Shouldn't we write a contract?"

"No need for contracts or promises from you. I trust in your honor!"

"But I am sorry, I don't trust in yours!"

"Try me this time." He bowed a very low bow then disappeared.

☙

Scores of years have passed since that night, years in which I devoured books, became knowledgeable in the various sciences and arts, and lived with philosophers, literary writers, musicians, and photographers. I loved "knowledge" madly. I could not tolerate being ignorant in any field. Sometimes I only had enough money needed for food till the end of the month, and yet if I came across a book or two displayed in a shop window I could not refrain from buying them with the money I had. For the rest of the days, I would drink the water of boiled rice and brewed tea leaves. My obsession went as far as making me desire to peruse what a literary writer does not have to read; thus I read books on astrology, spiritual sciences, and advanced mathematics.

My days off were spent in art galleries, natural history museums, libraries, and museums of antiquities.

I sat for long hours alone in a corner in a café; I would ponder for six or seven hours over abstruse matters of pure philosophy, intellectual issues, or economic, social, or political problems of the world. How many times have I destroyed cities in my head, and built instead imaginary civilizations with utopian systems just as Plato and Thomas More had done. How many times have I become a heretic and then a believer, lost faith and then regained it. How many times have I written and then torn up what I wrote. How ardently have I strived to reach that supreme pleasure that I thought was man's ultimate desire. I adored light and lived for its sake until I felt my body had become frail and my soul had wings like the wings of butterflies. I became like air, or like the angels, staying up late lost in thought over an open book under a lighted lamp. When morning came, I would lie down and escape from people and noise until an old maidservant eventually drew my attention to this, saying, "This life of yours is no life. Look at your face in the mirror."

I was horrified when I looked closely into the mirror of the wardrobe.

"What are all these wrinkles around my eyes? What is this back that is bent and hunched? What is this thinness and paleness? Did I forget my body all these years? Or did the devil make me pay the price without my knowledge?" I was flabbergasted by my appearance as I laid my finger on the frightful wrinkles on my face, seeming to indicate that the flower of life had gone forever. I could not help crying, "Youth! Youth! He took my youth!"

19

Resurrection at the Hands of Young People

Creative young people are those who resurrect their past. They provide their predecessors with new blood, which enables them to live in a new age. This is what the following passage from *The Book of the Dead* of the ancient Egyptians symbolizes:

> Horus: "Arise, arise Osiris!
> I am thy son Horus
> I have come to restore thee to life,
> I have come to collect thy bones,
> Tie together thy muscles
> And connect thy organs
> I am Horus of whom thou art the father
> Horus gives thee eyes to see with,
> Ears to hear with, feet to walk with,
> And arms to work with.
> Here are thy whole organs
> And thy body grows
> And thy blood runneth in thy veins.
> Thou shall always have thy true heart,
> Thy heart of old."
> The dead Osiris: "I am alive, I am alive!"
> (From *The Book of the Dead*)[1]

1. This is my (Radwan's) translation of this passage from *The Book of the Dead.*

Horus is none other than the "young people" restoring life to their dead past. Yes, he represents young people whose father is the homeland and to whom they gave eyes to see their great past with its freedom and their humiliating present in the chains of strangers, ears to hear the cynical laughs from the mouths of cowards who came to take advantage of their sleep and plunder their wealth, feet to walk with to prove to them that they are alive, and arms to rebuild the ruined edifice. All the organs of the homeland are sound and none of them are missing. Its body is moving and growing blood is running through its veins and at the head of it the young people cry out, "You will always have your real heart . . . your heart of old!"

It seems to me that I hear the homeland respond to the young people's call from every direction: "I am alive, I am alive!" I always believe that Egypt cannot die, as Egypt since time immemorial has kept on working and laboring for thousands of years with one goal: to fight death. Egypt has gained the object of its desire. Every time death thought it was victorious, Horus, one of its sons, would rise, shouting, "Arise, arise, homeland! You have your heart, always your real heart, and your heart of old." Thus death retreats on hearing the voice echoing from the depths of the homeland: "I am alive . . . I am alive!"

20

The Case of the Twenty-First Century

An American journalist visited me not long ago and said that he was visiting many countries to investigate why the whole world hates the United States. I looked at him closely while he took out a small notebook from his pocket to jot down my answers. He was a young man of less than forty years of age, tall and broad shouldered, like heroes in American movies. I had thought that such men were not to be found except in those days, but here I was seeing them in the flesh among male journalists, men growing in new soil, like stems of corn growing here in Egypt producing "early crop" in fertile soil. I did not let him wait long for my answer, for it did not require much thought as the Vietnam War with all its horror was vivid in our minds. I immediately told him that the world hates the United States as they believe it is responsible nowadays for igniting wars. Wherever it goes in Asia, Africa, the Far East, and the Middle East, one finds the matchbox in America's hands, playing with it or solving her problems with it, leaving the smoke to fill the peaceful sky. He wrote this down in his notebook, then raised his head to say, "Do you think that America can solve her problems without these wars?"

I said with clear conviction, "That is her message." He was surprised and impressed by the idealism in this word, so he jotted it down quickly. Then he turned towards me and said, "That's great. But from a practical point of view . . ."

I told him, "I am talking from a practical point of view. The message of peace in the hands of a powerful country is the best practical solution to all problems. If a powerful nation wants to be popular and to win the hearts of the world, it should put down the matchbox and release a dove of peace, this dove with two wings: a wing that stands for justice and the other for freedom."

"Thank you."

He said this as he was folding his notebook and inserting it in his pocket, and rose to say farewell. He left and I thought this was the end of the matter. Two days passed, and on the third day he came back to tell me that he had thought a great deal about the mission of a powerful nation in our present age and its responsibilities towards humanity. He wanted to investigate this issue seriously and asked for my assistance. I asked him, "Assist you in what?"

"In carrying out this mission."

When he saw my astonishment, he quickly said, "Of course the problem is not so easy. A great nation like the United States is not one person you can negotiate with. It is a structure that is full of contradictions and is extremely complicated. Have you ever been to the United States?"

I replied, "No, and I don't want to!"

"But you must want to, especially now. Listen. What would you say if I accompanied you there? It would not cost you anything. I would pay for your trip door to door. Don't use your old age or your health as excuses, as I said, for I'll provide you with every means of comfort. One of my relatives is also one of the counselors of the American president. He can arrange a visit for you to the White House so that you can personally discuss this important issue with the president."

"Keep away from me! Please!" I said this kindly and with a smile but in a firm tone.

Nevertheless he did not give up but insisted. Trying to persuade me, he said, "It is your mission too. You're the one who talks about missions. It is neither a visit for tourism nor an outing. The anxious world today is in need of thinkers who believe. If you really believe in a certain mission, you must exert some effort when you have the chance. Come on, give me your passport, and I'll prepare everything for you and book us tickets on the plane."

I could not help laughing. "So quickly? Am I a suitcase to be carried away like that?"

"And why should we procrastinate?"

"Are you afraid that the ailing world will perish before we arrive there? And what am I in all this? Whoever hears you will think I am a doctor flying with a cure!"

"Anyone who believes in a good idea is in a way a doctor. Let's go. Don't waste time. You won't lose anything by making this journey. Your new eye could discern at a glance the future of our society."

I thought for a while then said, "I can't stay there for more than a week."

"That will be enough."

"And no need to visit the White House. I don't meet heads of state."

"As you wish."

I quickly found myself being pushed hard to go on this journey. He prepared everything in the blink of an eye. I suddenly was at the airport. Then I was on the plane, with the damn journalist sitting next to me smiling. I could not believe what I had let myself in for. How did all this happen? The air hostess passed by with some candy, but I declined. I remembered that candy and certain airplane meals would not be healthy for me. But it was too late by then. There was no point in thinking about it. My friend the journalist reached out for some while looking thoughtfully at the hostess's pretty face saying, "She has beautiful eyes!"

I did not pay any attention to him and pretended to be asleep. My mood suddenly became worse and I was filled with depression for being uprooted in this way from my country, my home, and my habits to find myself on a crazy journey with no clear objective. How had he been able to convince me? This was not the first time I had been invited to visit his country or many other countries. I had been too lazy and lacked the enthusiasm to travel. So what had happened this time? Did I fall into the trap of the word I had uttered, "mission"? Now I was talking to myself and no one heard my inner voice:

"Was I serious when I uttered such words? Of course I was serious but not to the extent that I should bear such hardships for their sake at my age. How embarrassing? Thank God no one could hear me! Why did I blame myself when I actually responded to the appeal? But what appeal? How did I know it was not more than a press visit just like any other that journalists and writers are invited to? And perhaps this young journalist had invited other people before me in the same way. Everyone was tempted in the way that most suited him. It was too late to do anything, but I would not write a word about that visit or that country. I could see the headlines, 'Young journalist fools writer in his seventies and drags him from one plane to another!'"

When my thoughts reached this point, the journey seemed like hell and the journalist sitting next to me seemed like a devil. I could not bear to look at him, and my agony and stress increased and I wished to retrace my steps, enter my home, and throw myself on my comfortable bed. However, the plane was in the air and there was nothing left for me but to feel regret and repeat the proverb, "You have only yourself to blame when you listen to children."

ɞ

Throughout the journey, I said very little to the journalist. Whenever I noticed that he wished to talk, I pretended to be asleep. Thus he resorted sometimes to reading and other times to flirting with the air hostesses. When the journey was nearing its end, he called out, "We are now flying over the Statue of Liberty."

I sat up at once, leaning forward to look from the window. But it was nighttime so I could not see anything. I recalled what I had read about this huge statue. It was a gift from France to the United States, made by the French sculptor Bartholdi, who named it "Liberty Enlightens the World." It was erected by the United States in New York harbor in 1886. Yes, doubtless people's faith in America at that time was immense. The world expected that freedom would truly shine from America onto the world.

The plane landed at last, coming to a halt on the tarmac. It was not long before I was in the hotel that the journalist had chosen for me in New York. I was exhausted, so I went straight to my room and ordered a light supper and went to bed. I woke up early in the morning and ordered a cup of tea. Then I dressed and went down to the lobby to wait for my friend the journalist so we could set the program of my visit and begin our first day. I caught sight of the morning newspapers in the hands of some hotel guests bearing the large headline "The Statue of Liberty." I imagined, from the whispers and conversations around me, that I heard the words "Disappearance or robbery" or something of the sort. I told myself that was impossible, for the Statue of Liberty was not a needle that could disappear, nor a toy that could be stolen. There must be a mistake. My understanding of English, particularly American English, could lead me to misinterpret it. Soon my friend the journalist appeared holding a morning newspaper that he was absorbed in reading. As soon as he saw me he came towards me, greeted me, and said, pointing to the newspaper, "Imagine . . . the Statue of Liberty!"

"What? Did it disappear?" I said in a tone that astonished him. But he went on, "It seems it is the most important case of the season. I have been absent from the United States for about three months traveling around the world only to come back to find this strange case!"

"Can you put it in a nutshell?"

"Here, read it yourself!"

I took the newspaper from his hand and skimmed the headlines so I could find out what the main story was. There were four large photographs of two men and two women in their thirties or a little younger surrounded by a large picture of the Statue of Liberty. There was a headline in a large font: "A violent dispute between the prosecutor general and the defense over determining the crime." Then another heading: "Today the court will announce its decision regarding the exact charge." Another headline read, "Are the defendants criminals or reformers?" I did not continue reading, for I felt drawn to the case. I addressed my friend: "Can we attend the trial?"

"If you wish. As long as I am with you, everything will be fine."

"Let's go then!"

❧

We headed to the court. My friend the journalist did not need to show his identity card for he was well known there. The doors were quickly opened to us and we found ourselves inside the court room. The judge had not yet appeared, for his seat was still vacant, but the members of the jury were in their seats, as were the public. We were seated in one of the rows for the public. I looked at the place where the defendants would be and found the four young people whose photos I had seen in the newspapers. Addressing them were two men whom I realized were their defense team. Barely a minute later, the judge entered and took his seat near the American flag. He opened the session with a briefing of the argument that took place in the previous session with regard to the naming of the charges and how long the argument was expected to continue. He suggested that in order to save time, the court should hear the witnesses and listen to an exposé of the charges and the evidence (of the prosecutor and the defendants) for or against the defendants, from all of which the charge could be determined. At this point, one of the defense lawyers stood up. "In that case, the defendants are being detained without charge. Therefore, I demand their immediate release until the facts and evidence are clear and the court is able to deduce and determine the charge."

The public prosecutor rose. "Objection! They were caught red-handed."

The defense lawyer replied, "Caught red-handed doing what?"

"An act of sabotage."

"Is there any evidence that the intention of sabotage was in their minds?"

"What then was in their minds?"

"Shifting the statue from its present site, as they said in their testimony."

"Then it is robbery."

"You cannot describe it as robbery as it lacks the intention to possess."

"Where did they want to move the statue to?"

"A place that befits its meaning . . . The statue's meaning is liberty that enlightens the world. They wanted to transport it to a place where freedom shines."

The judge intervened, saying, "In this way we'll have endless contentions. I am forced to settle this disagreement and consider the charge of attempting to vandalize public property. The defense can try to prove otherwise. That is my decision; let us now hear the prosecution witnesses."

The public prosecutor smiled triumphantly. The defense attorney rose to address the judge. "Your honor, can you postpone this session for a few hours? . . . For your decision came as a surprise to us."

The judge agreed to adjourn the session until the afternoon. He stood up and left, and the audience dispersed. The journalist and I went to have lunch in a restaurant near the courthouse after the journalist found out that I intended to go back to the hearing to follow the case. My interest in it was natural. He understood, just as I did, that behind this case there was a greater and more profound issue. We drank our coffee, looked at the clock, and then rose to go back to the courthouse. We took our seats and the session resumed. The judge called the first witness. A man with military bearing marched in. He was one of the guards of the Statue of Liberty. He was sworn in and sat in the witness box. The judge asked him to relate what he knew. He said, "On the night in question it was my shift. At around 3 a.m., I heard the sound of a motorboat. I looked through my binoculars and saw a man wearing swim trunks on the boat. A minute later, another man appeared in the water wearing a diving suit followed by two women also in diving suits, all holding a long rope. They all climbed into the boat. I became suspicious and shouted at them and fired my gun in the air to prevent them from getting away. My colleagues came, and we searched the boat and found an explosive device. Then we brought divers to check the end of the long rope, and we discovered dynamite tied to the bottom of the rock that the statute is erected on."

Here the judge asked him to identify the defendants, and he pointed them out. The judge then showed him the evidence, namely, the sticks of dynamite, the rope, and the detonator, and the guard identified them. The judge referred the witness to the prosecution for questioning. He asked, "What was the defendant's objective in your point of view?"

"To blow up the statue, of course!"

"What did you deduce from the fact that they started the motor of the boat?"

"That the defendants were preparing to flee in the boat as soon as they boarded it and would press on the detonator's button."

"Then the disaster could have taken place if you had not heard the sound of the motor?"

"Certainly."

"Thank you."

The prosecutor turned to the jury. "As you see it is obvious that the defendants intended to blow up the statue and were actually carrying out their plan. They almost succeeded in what they had plotted. There was no other possibility."

He left the witness to be examined by the defense. One of the defense lawyers asked, "Where exactly did the defendant tie the sticks of dynamite?"

"At the bottom of the rock, in the water."

"This amount of dynamite is enough to cause damage to the bottom of the rock under the water. But is it enough to destroy the statue whose height is 93 meters above the water level?"

"I do not know. I am not an expert."

"Visitors can enter the building of the statue and climb up inside it. Wasn't it possible for the defendants to leave the explosives there or conceal a time bomb inside it?"

"There is strict security."

"Can this deter whoever wishes to try?"

"Of course not . . ."

"Therefore it was possible had they so wished?"

"Yes."

"Why did you fire the shot in the air?"

"To stop them from getting away."

"Did they show any sign that they wanted to flee or did you imagine it?"

"The sound of the running engine indicated to me that their boat was about to set off."

"Did you hear the sound of the motor as the boat approached the statue when they arrived?"

"No, because I was far away."

"Are you sure that the engine was silent and they started it to be ready to set off?"

"I only heard the sound of the engine."

"Isn't it possible that it was running all the time?"

"It is possible."

"Why then did you decide that they wanted to flee?"

"As a precaution."

"On your part. But on their part, did they show any sign that they desired to get away?"

"No."

"Thank you."

The prosecutor then said in a light mocking tone, "What aim does the defense wish to arrive at?"

The defense lawyer replied, "I wish to deny that our clients intended to flee, because they did not do anything that could be considered a crime. The witness was not certain that the dynamite under the rock was sufficient to sabotage the statue . . . and . . ."

The prosecutor interrupted him. "These matters require an expert and he is present in the court. Your honor, I beseech you to call the witness to come to the stand."

The judge summoned the witness who came forward, was sworn in, and sat in the witness box. He was shown the explosive devices, which he examined. The public prosecutor then asked him, "Did you examine the place where the dynamite was put?"

He answered, "Yes. It was ten meters below the water level."

"What is the extent of the damage that could have been caused to the edifice of the statute by the dynamite?"

"The damage cannot be precisely determined, though the explosion would have undoubtedly caused a serious tremor in the edifice."

"Is it possible that this serious tremor could lead to the collapse of the statue?"

"Everything is possible in that case."

"What do you think was the aim of this act?"

"Sabotage, of course."

"Couldn't there be another reason for this action, such as moving the statue from one place to another, for example?"

"Moving it from one place to another! A statue as large as this! And in such a childish way? That's a joke!"

"Then the seriousness of this hypothesis cannot occur to anybody, especially those who are highly educated and cultured like the defendants, who graduated from Harvard University with highest grades."

"To think in such a way, I believe, can in no way be serious because the project of moving such a statue from its site is a complicated technical operation that only a major engineering company can undertake."

The prosecutor turned to face the jury and said, "I think that you are now convinced that there was no other objective for the defendant apart from sabotage."

One of the lawyers stood up to ask the witness, "Can sabotage occur as soon as the dynamite is installed?"

"I did not understand the question."

"Can this dynamite cause an explosion simply by being installed as in the case of time bomb?"

"No, of course not. The detonator must be pressed."

"What if it was not pressed or there was no intention of pressing it?"

"In that case."

At this point, the prosecutor was roused to say, "What is the point of this? Is the defense trying to make us believe that the defendants installed the dynamite and sat in front of the detonator waiting for the guards to arrest them?"

The defense immediately replied, "That is exactly what happened." The defense then turned to the jury and added, "If our clients had the intention of sabotage, they would have immediately pressed the detonator before the guards arrived. They had enough time to do so."

The prosecutor commented sarcastically, "What was the intention of your clients? To move the statue from one place to another?"

The defense replied calmly, "The idea of moving the statue does not mean movement in the physical sense but in the symbolic and figurative sense. We are facing a new generation that is pure, intellectual, and upright and sees the statue 'Liberty Enlightens the World' in its present site and society as both a lie and a falsehood!"

The prosecutor stated, "This pure, innocent generation resorted on that day to sabotage."

Upon this, a cry of protest rang out from the defendant and the judge banged his gavel demanding silence. The defendants whispered with their defense team for a moment, then one of their lawyers rose up, headed towards the judge, and said, "With our clients' consent, we ask the court to hear them as witnesses."

The judge turned to the prosecutor and asked, "Does the prosecution have any objection?"

He answered, "No. No objection."

The judge declared, "Then this hearing is adjourned to ten o'clock tomorrow morning to hear the testimony of the defendants."

He stood up and left the bench. We all rose up and left the courtroom, heading to the street.

ẟ

My friend the journalist asked me about that night's program. He made a number of suggestions that did not appeal to me, as staying up late exhausts me. Moreover, I did not undergo the hardship of traveling there to enjoy nightlife or to go to theaters, clubs, or parties. My intention was to become acquainted with ideas, thoughts, and mentalities. I began to sense that this case was what I sought and desired, and it began gradually to reveal the heart of what we were looking for and needed to know about the true nature of this society: the problems of the age fermenting beneath it and boiling over. So let us devote ourselves to this case. Therefore it would be better for me to go to sleep early so I could wake up energetic and alert. I had something to eat and walked a little with my friend for exercise before I went to sleep. The lights of shops and nightclubs in the streets of New York were bursting with brilliant signs of various intermingling colors that sparkled and glittered to catch the eye before they grab what is in your pockets after a hard day's work. This is the consumer society they speak of. It is a huge human wheel that revolves all day to endlessly pour the sweat of its brow into its spring, this constant spring that never dries up, but where does its surplus go? Herein lies the question. I went back to my hotel and read a little in bed until I felt drowsy and fell asleep. I woke up in the morning and found that the newspapers had printed in large letters the news that the defendants would testify in that day's session. When it was around ten o'clock, my friend the journalist and I were in the courtroom. Members of the public took their seats in the room. The judge entered, and the important session that people were waiting for began. The first defendant was called to the witness stand and the judge asked him to give his testimony.

He said, "The four of us have been friends ever since we studied at Harvard University. My male companion and I were in the same department in the faculty of economics while my two female colleagues were in the department of humanities and philosophy. We only met them at the club around the swimming pool where we all competed in diving. After he and I graduated with honors, we were able to find good jobs in large companies. Then we were conscripted during the war in Vietnam. There we chanced to meet our two female friends who were working in one of the units. The four of us used to meet from time to time and chat, and we were struck by the similarity of our views and feelings about the hideous and loathsome reality in which we were living. We began to ask ourselves what the point was of it all. When we came back, we decided to do something that would make the world listen to us. We could not find a better platform than the courthouse for this purpose. We chose the Statue of Liberty to be the introduction to a public issue. We prepared everything very carefully to make it seem like sabotage. In such a way, we would go to court and have our say and our words would be published in the various news media. And that is what happened."

At this point, the judge turned to the public prosecutor to ask him whether he wanted to question the witness. He stood up readily and said, "Of course there are a lot of questions to be asked concerning such skill and innocence with which the defendant would like to depict the crime. It is best to deal with the facts in chronological order. I want you first to describe your family life."

The defendant replied in a slightly mocking tone, "My family life is very ordinary. There is nothing unusual about it. My father did not divorce my mother. And my mother did not let me wander aimlessly in the streets. In other words, I am a young man who cannot be described as what these days is called a deviant."

The prosecutor retorted, somewhat annoyed, "No one mentioned the word deviant. I asked you an ordinary question so you would give a simple answer. Nevertheless, I shall assume that you have answered. I'll ask you another question: What large company did you work in after graduation?"

"Portheed Company for Steel. I was in the financial department."

"Were they satisfied with you as an employee?"

"Yes, but I was not satisfied with my job after discovering the strong link between the company and the Pentagon. And I understood why wars break out, and why hundreds of thousands of young Americans and millions of children, old people, and women die in Asia."

"Could you deduce that from working in your company?"

"Of course. The company's budget is part of my department specialization. And when I see over a billion dollars of contracts given by the military to a company that has influence in the government, it becomes easy to know who will benefit from the wars."

"Don't you know that democracy is the governing system in our country?"

"Yes, I do. But I also began to realize that monopolies and the military are the fingers inside the rubber gloves of democracy."

"Didn't you try to investigate the political reasons that made the Vietnam War a national necessity?"

"I investigated and asked, why don't we leave Asia to the Asians? What is the necessity to interfere there and prevent them from choosing the system they want for themselves? The answer was 'Their economic independence. We do not want them to be economically independent.'"

"Don't you know that their economic independence means the collapse of our national economy?"

"No, it means the collapse of the economy based on the monopolies that thrive and grow on the blood they drain from Asia and Africa and the food of the Asians and Africans."

"What does this matter to you?"

"It is important to me that these endless wars should be stopped because Asia and Africa have awakened and will defend their food, which is their life. But the monopolistic military alliance will not cease from snatching this food and this life and will not accept any decrease in its weight or rate of growth, because any decrease will not enable them to pay salaries that would satisfy their workers and profits that would satisfy their shareholders. It would then collapse, for it has to protect its life too. Therefore, there are wars into which we young people are thrown to die or to kill other peoples. Thus we make our society to be like a jungle where wild beasts kill each other to fill their bellies."

"So you want to change this society?"

"Yes, because it is against human dignity for such a society to survive until the next century."

"So you admit that you wanted to change this society? By which means then do you wish to change it? Through destruction and sabotage?"

"By destroying old ideas."

"Through violence?"

"No, we cannot support violence when we oppose war."

"Are you one of the young hippies?"

"I am one of the young people who oppose war and call for peace."

"That did not stop them from committing murder. What do you think of that?"

"Of course no young person would approve of this. If you mean those who murdered Sharon Tate and the massacre that took place in her home, we all shuddered when we read the defendant Manson's memoirs. He is a kind of Rasputin who is a mixture of Jesus and the devil and mixes heaven with blood. He is a unique type who does not represent anything or anyone. He represents nobody but himself."

"Don't you see the distasteful behavior of the young hippies as a sort of sabotage of society?"

"It is as if they're destroying themselves first and foremost. If they meant to destroy society by destroying themselves, it would be a sacrifice like other sacrifices. When they find that they have no choice but to die in wars for monopolistic capitalism or to die from a sense of loss caused by the hatred of these wars, both are the same to them."

"Then you accept sabotage, whether of the society or of the self?"

"I do not like to commit any crime of any sort."

"Did you ever take marijuana or any type of drugs?"

"No, and I don't like young people to resort to taking them whatever their motives. I believe only a small percentage of the millions of hippies take drugs, engage in public sexual intercourse, or commit such vileness that is exaggerated and publicized by those who want to oppose the young people's movement against war in order to disfigure the face of this revolution."

"Do you belong to this revolution?"

"Yes, I belong to every revolution that is against these dirty wars and those who ignite them whether they are monopolists or the military."

"Why is it that the young people are the ones who are carrying out this revolution?"

"Because they are the ones who will see the twenty-first century. They want to pass on to it a better society. That is the issue. We young people cannot permit this corrupt society to cross the threshold of the new century. We will do everything in our power to pave the way for the new century with new ideas, just as the French Revolution of the nineteenth century paved the way for new ideas and a new society and just like the nineteenth century paved the way with new socialist ideas."

"In your opinion, what will society be like in the next century?"

"It is difficult for the revolution to clearly see the image of a future society."

"Did the revolutionaries in France, for example, foresee the society thirty years on when they demolished the Bastille?"

"Then do you consider the demolition of the Bastille the most important step in the revolution?"

"It was a symbol . . . just a symbol."

"Like demolishing the Statue of Liberty?"

"We have not yet gone that far."

"What stage have you reached, then?"

"The seeds of the revolution have actually begun to grow in this society."

"Do you mean the revolt against the system of this society?"

"Yes."

"What is the difference between sabotage and revolt?"

"My two female companions can answer this question better than I can, as they studied the humanities and social sciences."

"When you were at college, were you a rebellious one?"

"No. I was an ordinary student."

"When did the idea of a revolution occur to you?"

"When we came back from Vietnam, as I said earlier."

"And what about the rest of the young people who didn't go to Vietnam, how did they begin to think of a revolution?"

"I don't know!"

"Are there any leaders directing this movement?"

"I have no idea."

"Which of you thought of sabotaging the Statue of Liberty?"

"We all thought of it at the same time."

"Who drew up the plan?"

"I did."

"And where did you get the dynamite and the detonator from?"

"My father works in a construction company, and I was able to get the materials from the company storehouses."

"With your father's knowledge?"

"No."

"You stole them, then?"

"I borrowed them. We had no intention, of course, of taking possession of or keeping them."

"I see. You always have good intentions! And who was it who placed the sticks of dynamite on the rock?"

"I did . . . with the help of my two female companions."

"What did your fourth companion do?"

"We left him in the boat because he isn't good at diving."

"And who was supposed to set off the detonator?"

"No one! As we told you, we had no intention of setting off the explosion."

"If this was truly your intention, why didn't you use empty sticks of dynamite or an inactive detonator?"

"We did actually consider this. But we realized that this farce would be immediately discovered, and thus the whole plan would be ruined and we wouldn't get the chance to appear in court."

"Now that you are in court, what is this vital message that you want to announce from this platform?"

"We want people to be definitely aware that there is now an issue, a serious issue, which is the case of the twenty-first century, the century that will not be characterized by aggression, racial or social discrimination, or capitalist monopoly. It will be the century of love, peace, and fraternity. The revolution has started within this aggressive and worn-out society and nothing will stand in its way until the glad tidings of a new society begin to appear. We call upon all people from where we stand to revolt with us against old ideas that are not valid for life in tomorrow's world. We also ask them to prepare themselves to accept the inevitable change, otherwise the coming generations will sweep them away with the garbage of the violated century."

"Do you have a clear idea as to how to change the present society?"

"I don't understand the question."

"The revolution that you said will change society: will it be a popular social revolution, a political parliamentary one, or a military coup?"

"It is impossible to imagine any of that happening in America."

"Then what is this revolution?"

"It is the revolution of new ideas for a new generation."

"Do you mean this generation of young people who are lost and wandering about like dirty stray dogs?"

"This generation is the sacrificial avant-garde. It is the firewood and fuel of the fire of the revolution that will devour worn-out ideas and values. Subsequently, young people will appear who will avenge the previous generation with their new ideas and new values that befit the twenty-first century."

"Is a revolution of ideas without violence effective enough?"

"Violence is not necessary in all cases to achieve major changes. A half-naked man in a cloth was able to expel a mighty empire from his country. That was the Indian leader Gandhi."

"Then do you think that the young people's revolution will be like Gandhi's?"

"I don't think this is how they picture the revolution now, especially the hippies who didn't study that man well enough. He too with his bare body and his goat didn't care for appearances, but his simple attire and his energy moved people to feel sympathy and respect and did not arouse the disgust that most young people's disrobing and obscene lack of restraint cause nowadays. That is why they lost a major part of their battle, because of their appearance. Moreover, the Central Intelligence Agency made use of this to turn public opinion against them, and they were harassed by silly, simple, and ignorant people."

"Do you believe that these young people have true faith in this revolution you are talking about?"

"I don't think the way they view the revolution now is like that of mature adults. Most of them are young. Revolution to them is spontaneous not ideological. They understand it as a way of life that should be different from the way of their predecessor. It is just how they feel about their new age. It is their feeling about the age that connects and unites them. The uniformity in dress and appearance among the Americans, Africans, and Asians today is a result of a strong sense of the age. Their age and the times influence young people all over the world in the same way regardless of the differences between societies and environments. This will undoubtedly eliminate racial and social discrimination in the future. But the revolution as faith in a specific doctrine is the work of leaders, thinkers, and legislators. This will happen at the right time."

"Don't you consider the departure from the limits of prevailing morals a type of sabotage?"

"It is not I who considers it so. It is the laws of the state that punish what they consider a kind of sabotage. The authorities, for example, arrest whoever takes drugs. Young people are not the only ones who take them; in fact statistics reveal that the number of drug addicts who are middle-aged, old, and senile is much greater than the number of young addicts. These middle-aged people are also the ones who grow, manufacture, and traffic all these narcotics. They are responsible."

"Do you mean that the older generations are responsible for what is happening?"

"It is self-evident. If the corruption doesn't stem from them, why would we need to revolt against them?"

"You claim that your revolution is nonviolent. Why then did you resort to a form of violence by trying to destroy a statue that is state property?"

"I have already said that sabotage wasn't our intention."

"I know that. But I'm not talking about intentions now. I'm talking about the way you behaved and the procedures you took. For example, if you were discussing with somebody the subject of love, freedom, and peace and then you took out a toy gun, which he imagined was real, wouldn't you have resorted to a kind of violent situation?"

"Of course. But in our case it is different. We did not want to threaten or frighten or influence anybody. We only wanted to find an excuse to enter the court to publicly discuss the issue of a coming age."

"Why couldn't there be another interpretation of that incident, which is that you wanted to make rebellious young people, who look at you, understand that resorting to a form of violence is possible or necessary as an effective measure when the need arises?"

"It never occurred to us that we could be models to young people in such matters."

"Do you think this absolves you from the responsibility?"

"I don't know."

"Do you know of a plan or intention on the part of young people to use violence in the future?"

"No, I don't."

"Do you think that the young people's revolution will inevitably resort to violence?"

"Not necessarily. All the signs so far show that it is a type of passive resistance, and if Gandhi was able to defeat the British Empire, then the young people's revolution can also defeat the capitalist American empire after it goes beyond the first stage, which is chaotic, instinctive, and spontaneous. Then this rushing torrent will begin to form a regular stream."

"Do you know of any leading organizations working in that direction and for that purpose?"

"No, I don't."

"But you don't rule out their existence or the thought of finding them?"

"That is very possible."

"Are there any particular writings that are directed to or have an influence on young people?"

"Young people who read will of course find in some writings what could influence them or perhaps what could help them to form their revolutionary ideology, but this would be a small percentage of young people. However, millions of them are still unaware of these writings. It is now, as I have said, in the stage of mobilization, unification, and spontaneous imitation of other revolutions in an instinctive revolutionary upsurge. This is a natural stage at the beginning of many historical revolutions, when the masses of people begin to surge forward impulsively with an indefinite objective or a general demand before they enter the stage of well-planned, clear, and organized revolutionary thought."

"Do you know any of the leaders of this revolution of the young?"

"No."

"If you knew any of them, would you tell us about them?"

"There would be nothing to stop me from doing so if I was not bound by a promise or an oath."

"In such cases, would there be any kind of restrictions or ban on freedom of speech?"

"I don't know. Not necessarily. But I mean that if any person asks you not to mention his name on one particular occasion or in any context however normal or trivial, then one should respect his wishes."

"Thank you."

❧

Saying this, the prosecutor ended questioning the witness. Then the judge turned to the lawyer of the defense and asked if he wanted to cross-examine his client before he stepped down from the witness stand. The defense declined, stating that he was satisfied with his client's testimony. The judge was then about to adjourn the session.

Just before the judge could do so, the defense counsel requested that next day's session be to hear the second defendant's testimony. The judge consented and rose to leave. Everyone stood up and left the courtroom, as did the journalist and I. We walked in silence thinking of what we had heard. To be more accurate, I was in deep thought while he kept glancing at me, as if trying to seize the chance to find out my opinion. The more aware I was of his intention, the longer I remained silent, to stop him from asking questions. We entered one of the restaurants. Then we came out to find that some newspapers had come out with various headlines in large print, some of which were "Today's exciting session," while some declared, "Revolution in America," and others, "The Left sweeps through the young." We seized the newspapers and became absorbed in reading the conflicting comments on what we had seen and heard all day.

ꟷ

(2)

My friend the American journalist tried again to tempt me to discuss the testimony of the witness that day and find out what I thought of it. We were sitting in the hotel cafeteria drinking coffee. He jotted down some points in his small notebook from time to time. I knew that he would be writing about the case for his newspaper. It was impossible for a journalist to spend all this time in a courtroom listening to a case that was shaking the country and not write an article about it. But what kind of article would he write? There were the comments in the newspapers, mostly revolving around the ability of young people to bring about a real change in American society. Some of them dealt with young people's revolt with slander, sarcasm, and distortion. Some showed keen interest in what was mentioned in that day's hearing about "passive resistance" while other reports were filled with anxiety. There was no doubt that this peaceful weapon had succeeded in India at the hands of Gandhi. Some newspapers showed special interest in the defendant's testimony that if Gandhi was able to defeat the British Empire through passive resistance then there was nothing to stop the new generations from defeating the American empire with the same weapon. But the question that was repeated was whether the spirituality of Gandhi and India had the greater effect in that victory.

Do young Americans have the same spirituality? Or can this weapon be used in any country and any age? If we remember that "passive resistance" is not Indian, and that Gandhi admitted—with the rare gift of greatness—that he had borrowed it from Tolstoy, and that what grew in Russian soil was imported and planted in Indian soil, then it is also possible that the idea could be transferred from a country in the East to one in the West and could grow and produce the same fruit.

All the above comments with their various directions express a worry with America's destiny only. Nevertheless, the defendant spoke in his testimony about something the newspapers did not focus sufficiently on, with his reference to the twenty-first century and his statement that the issue was really of that century and that any form of aggression should be prevented from extending to it. It was therefore the mission of young people all over the world not just American youth. This is because the next century belongs to every young person on Planet Earth regardless of color or race. Moreover, every young person on earth, from the east to the west, is responsible for preparing for the new century that he or she will live in alone without parents and predecessors. The testimony of the first defendant that day made this clear. What would the second defendant testify tomorrow? My eagerness was intense. How I wished the next day would come quickly so that I would find myself in court. I left my journalist friend to go to his workplace and finish his article and we agreed to meet the next morning. I remained in my hotel room.

Morning came, and we walked together to the courthouse. The session began. The judge asked the second defendant to take the witness stand. She was a young woman of a little under thirty, moderately pretty, wearing eye glasses behind which appeared a piercing and intelligent gaze, and with tastefully coiffed blond hair. There was nothing unusual, outstanding, or abnormal in her appearance. This was also true of all the other defendants. There was nothing that attracted one's attention in their outward appearance. From the start, our attention was directed to their words not their appearance.

The judge invited her to testify and she stated simply and briefly, “I have nothing much to add to my companion’s testimony except that after my companion and I graduated from the College of Humanities with honors, we were appointed to jobs in the Library of Congress where we remained until we were summoned to Vietnam. Upon our return to the States, all four of us met and began to think of the fate of the age in which we live and what we should do to improve matters, as my companion stated earlier.”

She fell silent. Thereupon, the prosecutor asked the judge’s permission to question the defendant, which was granted. He said, “I will not burden the witness with questions about her family and upbringing. It is obvious that we are facing a type of young people who are not deviant in morals and behavior, but are deviant in mind and thought. It is odd that the defendant should be living among books in a great library like the Library of Congress and would think of taking part in a crime of sabotage. That is why I would like to ask her whether she did not feel at any time the error of what she was about to do.”

She calmly replied, “I didn’t feel that there was anything wrong. The only wrong thing, in our point of view, is to keep quiet about the errors of this age.”

“And were the errors of the age only revealed to you during the Vietnam War?”

“This war, as well as the others, is a result of these errors.”

“And in your point of view, can you fix these mistakes through crime?”

“Of course not.”

“Then why did you and your accomplices resort to sabotage?”

“We did not intend sabotage.”

“Then what did you intend?”

"We intended to stop the mistakes of this century from extending to the next one. I thought a lot about this while I was working in the Library of Congress. When I was revising the indexes, some books seemed to me to be responsible for many catastrophes, such as those that glorify wars and those that worship people the likes of Alexander, Julius Caesar, and Napoleon. I thought it would be best to destroy these books so that they would not reach the coming generations. I thought of setting fire to the section that holds these books in the Library of Congress."

"Setting fire to them? And how were you planning to set fire to the Library of Congress?"

"What is the meaning of this question?"

"Did you think, for example, of using dynamite or a time bomb to be planted in one of the corners of the Library of Congress?"

At this juncture, the defense leaped up, shouting, "I object! The prosecutor is making use of my client's poor defense and her ill-chosen expression, which was a casual slip of the tongue, to turn it into a new accusation to bind her with."

The public prosecutor replied, "I am not making a new accusation. But since the defendant's statement indicated her intention of sabotage, I must follow up this idea."

He turned to the judge for his opinion, and the latter signaled to him to continue questioning the defendant. So he turned back to the defendant, asking her, "Did you tell any of your partners of the idea that occurred to you to set fire to the Library of Congress?"

"I only told my companion. She laughed. We both laughed and didn't take the matter seriously after that."

"Did you laugh at the idea because it was difficult to implement?"

"We never thought of implementing it."

"How then did you think of committing the other crime, which is sabotaging the Statue of Liberty?"

"We have already said that we did not intend to commit it. We only meant to act as if it were a crime without actually carrying it out."

"And when you thought of setting fire to the Library of Congress did you also mean not to carry out the actual act of arson?"

"And why not?"

"This is not a proper answer to be given in court. We want a clear and definite answer."

"The idea of setting fire to the Library of Congress was a stupid idea and the result of a sudden provocation."

"And what is the difference between setting fire to the Library of Congress and setting fire to the Statue of Liberty?"

"Burning books is in all cases a barbaric act, whatever type of books they may be or the extent of harm they cause."

"And how do you prevent these harmful books from reaching the coming generations?"

"By revolting against them."

"What is the connection between revolution and sabotage?"

"There doesn't always have to be a connection between revolution and sabotage. There is sabotage without revolution. There is also a revolution without sabotage."

"How can there be a revolution without sabotage?"

"Sabotage is sabotage. And revolution is the will for change. The will for change may rise and the change may actually take place without sabotage or violence. My companion has already mentioned something about passive resistance, which is the weapon of a peaceful revolution. The revolution may also break out too without any resistance at all. If the public feeling wants and supports it, then there will be nothing to stand in its way."

"But it is rare that a revolution can take place without violence."

"Violence occurs when there is opposition to the revolution, that is, if there is a force that counters the will for change and tries to repel it with violence. The revolution in turn is then certain to make its way with the same violence, for violence breeds violence."

"Why did you think then of using violence at the beginning of your so-called revolution?"

"We've already said we only meant to attract attention."

"Why should attracting attention be achieved through crime?"

"I have just said that it is not a crime but merely the semblance of a crime."

"Isn't the semblance of violence a kind of terrorism?"

"We didn't have terrorism in mind."

"Anyway, it is an admission by you of the value of violence."

"We are against the use of violence."

"But enacting the part, as you all have said, and perfecting the part is conclusive evidence that you didn't rule it out from your calculations."

"It is just a hoax."

"Isn't the resort to simulation proof that you are in need of it? And the mere simulation of a crime is useful to you in carrying out your activities?"

"Unfortunately, we live in a society in which nothing attracts its attention like the appearance of a crime or the sight of a crime or a scene of deviation."

"What is the cause of your hostility and revolt against this society?"

"My companion has already spoken about this. I see no reason why I should repeat it. But I don't mind if I reaffirm what he said, that this society isn't fit for future life, for it is drugged.

It is in need of a jolt to awaken it, to realize that it is always dreaming in old images at a time when the astronaut heralds the beginning of new thoughts. This society isn't shocked or surprised to see politicians and leaders who still dream of the influence of bygone empires, or rulers and countries that still dream of repeating the glory of kings in the Old Testament. It wonders at, mocks, and accuses young people of being primitive when they let their hair grow long and walk about naked! Such a society that sees abnormality in trivialities and doesn't see or oppose it in the minds and dreams that lead to disasters is a society that doesn't deserve to live in the next century."

"Then you want to destroy images of the past in society?"

"We want the society to be worthy of its age and to freely contemplate all the images and values to analyze them in the light of the present and the future in order to retain what it can to build a new humanity in the new space age."

"And who has the right to judge the images and values? You?"

"We as well as others, even middle-aged and old people, whoever was able to free his mind and thoughts from the gravitational force of Mother Earth's inherited customs and deeply embedded ideas."

"Then you want to destroy the values and ideas that society lives by?"

"We want to say that in the age of the new human being, there are no indisputable ideas and everything should be reconsidered."

"Don't you think that there should be some indisputable ideas that society could lean on, and whoever destroys them would be like one who destroys the foundations of a house on the pretext of rebuilding it?"

"We actually do want to rebuild society."

"Doesn't rebuilding it require demolition first?"

"Naturally."

"Thank you!"

The prosecutor moved away from the defendant and turned towards the jury. "We have finally reached the natural outcome, which is proof of the intention of demolition and sabotage on the part of these defendants. This defendant has admitted before you that to destroy society with the claim of rebuilding it is something natural. Therefore if they claim that the intention for sabotage wasn't present when they placed the dynamite under the statue and prepared to blow it up with an active detonator that was about to be set off and cause destructive damage, if they so claim and try to convince us that they had good intentions, should we believe them? If we remember the defendant's contemplation of setting fire to the Library of Congress, should we believe her?"

The jury kept scrutinizing the face of the defendant as she sat in the witness box, calm and composed. Her defense lawyer stood and asked to question her. The judge granted permission, stating that the session would take place in the afternoon at the defense's request so as not to exhaust his client. The session was adjourned. My friend the journalist and I left to have coffee and sandwiches and then went for a walk in the streets. Newspapers had come out bearing the big dramatic headline of "The burning of the Library of Congress!"

The streets also were full of exciting aspects that make one wonder and think. At every turn, we came across groups of people carrying signs bearing strange and sometimes contradictory slogans. Some were calling for equality between whites and blacks. Some were calling for the annihilation of black people, and some were calling for the prevention of wars, and some were calling for the legalization of sexual deviation. Some commended the domination of men over women, while others sanctioned the domination of women over men. There were all forms imaginable of clamor, convulsions, and spasms that reveal a psychologically disturbed society. My friend the journalist passed by all of that and did not look surprised, as if it were an ordinary everyday scene. But it was different for me, for I who came from afar began to glimpse in all that I observed a warning of something that will happen, the features of which are not easy to determine at this point.

The time came to return to the courthouse. We went back and sat in our usual seats and soon the session began. The second defendant took her place on the witness stand. The judge gave her lawyer permission to begin questioning her. The lawyer asked, "When you said you wanted to destroy society in order to rebuild it, did you mean material or moral destruction?"

The defendant immediately replied, "Moral destruction, of course."

"Did you mean that you in particular and your companions were entrusted with this destruction and construction?"

"No, that is not what I meant when I say we want to demolish or reform society; we are using a style of expression that is synonymous with saying 'we hope' or 'we foresee' because this task is beyond our means. The only thing we can do and what we wanted to achieve was to convey a message or a warning or direct people's attention."

"Then your action was like someone lighting flame in the dark to alert people to something?"

"That is exactly what we wanted."

"And what you wanted to announce or alert them to was for the good of society?"

"Of course. Every diagnosis of the state of society is for its benefit. Today society is in a state of craving, indicating that it is pregnant with child. All the symptoms of strong craving are apparent today in the sense of nausea, continuous vomiting, bad temper, tension, anxiety, loss of appetite at times, and an appetite for deviance at other times. Carelessness, flabbiness, negligence, breaking down, complaints, screams, the feeling of suffocation, and the desire to be unrestrained. It is craving in its worst cases, which announces the movement of the fetus in the womb of a pregnant society."

"What do you mean by this fetus?"

"This fetus is the natural fruit of two events that are considered among the major events in human history. In fact, they are the biggest events that have happened to mankind throughout the ages: the bombing of Hiroshima and the landing of man on the moon. We weren't half-conscious of what had taken place and its outcome. We were totally unaware. If we review history, we'll find societies that were turned upside down by events that were less significant and less important, such as the discovery of gunpowder, steam, or electricity. But it always takes some time for these events to leave their trace in transforming a society, turning it upside down and changing it. This is what will inevitably happen."

"Let us go back to the image of the fetus. Do you think that this fetus will be born disfigured or normal?"

"I hope it will be normal."

"Isn't the revolt of young people one of its features?"

"I think it is one of the symptoms of craving in pregnancy. It is one of its signs, but it isn't the actual thing itself."

"Are you optimistic by nature?"

"I haven't studied my character well. Sometimes I am and sometimes I am not. But what matters to me is to try to foresee the future. Perhaps some of my own wishes may be realized as well as some of my deductions that were based on readings and observations."

"Do you read a lot?"

"Yes, I do. My companion and I spend most of the time reading and exchanging books. Our being together in the Library of Congress makes this easier."

"Do you think that tomorrow's society will be better than today's?"

"It will in all cases be the product of the age."

"Do you think it will be a scientific or a primitive society?"

"The difference between what is scientific and what is primitive is the methodology. What we call science is gaining knowledge through rational methodology and what we call primitive is to gain knowledge through unmethodological and irrational means. Our society is founded on mental science. There is nothing to prevent adding the path of primitive knowledge tomorrow."

"Is this therefore a regression to the past?"

"Not exactly. First we must find another word besides primitivism or the primitive. In reality, there is no beginning or end on this planet. The mental faculty coined that word, because it must work in a temporal or spatial sphere. Thus this machine must have two points: a departure point and an arrival point. But the planet or nature doesn't know that; it only knows continuous transformations and changes."

"Is there not then a forward movement?"

"Undoubtedly. When man chooses a path and walks in it, he is actually advancing. This is what happened to man when he chose to advance in the path of reason and made all these amazing inventions. Nevertheless, before man chose that path, there was also an amazing power in his formation: there was a radar inside him. He had very sharp sight, even for objects he could not see. He could control external objects with hidden sources of inner power. But one day it occurred to this man to use a tool with his hands, like the branch of a tree or a piece of rock. So he invented the knife and the spear. He discovered that he had a brain that thinks, creates, and invents. He began to enjoy this, so he used this rational instrument to invent one thing after another. He was enthralled with his inventions, became dependent on them, and forgot his original faculty so it withered and dwindled. He continued along in his path, creating, inventing, and discovering until he arrived at the present, the computerized, technological, and rational society that thinks and works for him."

"Then there is a danger facing our society that our mental faculty will wither?"

"Not so quickly and not so easily. But what happens from time to time is the awareness of and the search for other sources of knowledge apart from the methodological scientific mentality. For instance, some scientists are interested in the spiritual, in psychoanalysis and what is termed unconscious. Moreover, some artistic trends have appeared that try to explore the spontaneous sources in the arts of children or tribes that are close to the environment of early man."

"Don't you think that the revolt of young people is one of these signs?"

"It is very possible. Young people of course don't think about that so directly, but maybe the general atmosphere of our technological society provokes them to spontaneously desire to slip away from their orbit, either by returning to the environment of early man with his nakedness and social freedom or through freeing themselves from the moral responsibility by means of drugs that fling them out from our age."

"Do you think that young people of the world are united in this direction?"

"On the contrary. Each nation has its own unique conditions, and what applies to one society doesn't exactly apply to another. Young people themselves differ from one another. But my words are directed to a society like our technological capitalist society."

"Do young people around the world unite in certain things in spite of the differences in their societies, peoples, and races?"

"Yes! It is in the way they sense the spirit of the new age. It is the way young people all over the world feel regarding the unity of the age, the world, and the future that is liberated from what is antiquated and worn out."

"How can we reconcile the desire to break away from the antiquated and the desire to return to the primitive?"

"Primitivism isn't being antiquated. It is the eternal healthy instinct in man. If it was viewed from the accepted point of view of the arts, as I have said, whether the plastic or musical arts, it would mean something important. On the other hand, antiquated refers to the customs, traditions, and tastes that were preferred by predecessors who want to force them upon descendants just because they are older, like raising a hat to greet somebody as a form of politeness, shaving one's moustache or trimming hair as a duty, or appreciating a certain type of music, painting, sculpture, book, or literature as a sort of refinement."

"Do you like Picasso?"

"I do like Picasso, Kandinsky, and Paul Klee, because they studied the secrets of primitive African art. If Beethoven were alive, he would have been inspired by Negro music as he was by gypsy music in his seventh symphony, and as Shakespeare was influenced by clowns' jokes and obscenities. Great people see things as great while the small see them as small."

"What if primitive man had not chose the path of reason and had continued in the path of his other hidden powers, how far do you think he could have advanced?"

"I can't answer this question because I can't imagine man without the power of reason."

"Then you are for progress and not the destruction of progress?"

"Undoubtedly. But we must always determine the meanings of words. What is the meaning of progress? I've already mentioned that nature doesn't know anything but transformations and changes that are necessary and suitable for life. For example, if it understood progress as we do, it would have made the first cell grow in size steadily and regularly. The ant, for example, would lead to the mouse then to the cat, then the dog, then to man, then to the cow, and to the elephant until it came to the dinosaur today. But what happened was that this huge development in size came 70 million years before the relatively small human being. They are therefore transformations and changes according to surrounding circumstances. What we call the progress or mental expansion of man today may reach a limit tomorrow that would make it necessary for his life to bring about other transformations and changes."

"Is there any hope or way for man to regain some of the hidden primitive powers he has lost?"

"I think this happens in every age, for there are always attempts by those who are called magicians, priests, or indigent Indians—the real ones, of course, not the tricksters. Some of them, after long practice, mysticism, spiritual abstraction, or psychological transparency, attained some kind of control over distant objects and were able to move and transfer them through their inner powers alone without any material intervention."

"What if the whole human race was able to regain this hidden power?"

"This of course would be a wonderful thing, though I don't want to be around here to see it."

"Why not?"

"I imagine that I would not be happy in such a world where we have knowledge but do not create."

"Is the working of the brain a habit?"

"I don't know. But if I were given the choice of being a complete instrument of knowledge that does not create or an incomplete instrument that creates, I would prefer the second."

"Have you ever taken drugs?"

"No."

"Didn't you come across anybody who tempted you to try them?"

"Of course, I certainly did. But I resisted the temptation. I was afraid lest I fall captive to this habit."

"So you do observe moral values?"

"Of course—the values that deserve to survive."

"Then you have a conservative spirit?"

"Yes."

"How can the conservative spirit be reconciled with the destructive spirit?"

"I don't know."

"Thank you."

The defense turned towards the jury and said, "We now know that my client is in truth deep down a conservative. It is impossible for somebody like her to commit sabotage or aim at destruction. I don't need to say any more. Her answers are clear to you, and they cannot come from a person such as the prosecutor has described."

The defense returned to his seat. The judge noticed that the public prosecutor was silent and did not request to reexamine the defendant, so he signaled to her to step down from the witness stand. He adjourned the session to the next day.

We returned the next day to find a surprise awaiting us that shocked us and shocked the audience. The prosecutor brought a surprise witness and asked the court to hear his testimony. The witness was a priest.

He stated that the two male defendants came to him one day about three months earlier to ask him to join them in matrimony. Moreover, on the same day the two female defendants came to him to do the same thing, namely, to marry them. He refused to perform this kind of marriage uniting two people of the same sex. Then the prosecutor rose to question him. "Do you regard this kind of marriage as opposed to religion?"

He replied, "And against the laws of the state and the morals of society."

"What was the defendants' intention in taking that action?"

"I don't know. It is a deviant act in any case."

"Do they mean by this abnormal act to demolish moral values?"

"It is in fact demolition of moral values."

"Thank you." The prosecutor then commented, "What we have heard now from the priest definitely refutes what we heard yesterday from the defense about the defendant's observance of moral values. If the defendants have the audacity to practice such abnormal behavior that sabotages society's moral standards, then it is not surprising if they try to sabotage the Statute of Liberty, or set fire to the Library of Congress!"

At this point, the defense of the second defendant rose to ask that she be called to testify again. She rose up and sat in the witness box. He asked her, "You told us yesterday that you observe moral values, so how do you explain this act we have heard about now?"

She answered unhesitatingly, "What I said exactly was that I observe moral values that are worthy of survival."

"And what is the measure of what is worthy and what isn't worthy of survival?"

"What is not worthy of survival is what remains after the reasons for it to disappear."

"Did the reasons for the marriage of males and females disappear?"

"Of course not. But the reasons for the prohibition of marriage between people of the same sex have disappeared."

"How did this happen? Please clarify this point."

"We must ask first, why was marriage between male and female legalized? The main reason of course was to create offspring. In the past, procreation was a blessing. Today procreation is a curse because the population explosion threatens the world with disaster. In such a society that survived for thousands of years, all the legislation was based on protecting and encouraging procreation. It was therefore natural that marriage be understood to lead to procreation and thus could not occur without the coupling of male and female. Every other union that did not lead to procreation was combatted for fear of a decrease in the birthrate. It was the age where propagation was the pride of families, tribes, and nations. But today things are different. After the procreative society, we have become a society of birth control, so why should we prohibit marriages that don't lead to procreation? If the reasons for the prohibition no longer exist, why should the prohibition remain?"

"And why did you want to marry your companion?"

"It was our mutual wish."

"Was it for sexual intercourse?"

"If it was for sexual intercourse, our relationship would have continued secretly and there would not have been any need to announce it. But we wanted our relationship to have a legal basis to confirm and show our desire for the need to reconsider the reasons and bases of laws."

"Did all four of you go to get married at the same time based on a prior agreement?"

"Yes. The idea occurred to us and so we carried it out together."

"Did you mean to defy the laws?"

"No, we just wanted to draw attention to the fact that the reasons for these laws have disappeared. And that our age should reconsider the matter."

"And why did you choose the law of marriage in particular?"

"Because it is the one that draws the most attention. There is another law that is less important, namely, the ban on abortion while at the same time contraceptives are encouraged. Could it be more contradictory? But society is too cowardly to annul an old prohibition."

"What do you think are the reasons behind this cowardice of society?"

"Its fear of discussing accepted ideas. And its inability to free itself from old customs."

"Then your intention was to call for the discussion of accepted ideas and customs?"

"Yes."

"But the prosecution considers this act a kind of undermining of society's moral values?"

"If there are no free discussions of the accepted ideas and customs, how will humanity change from one society to another? Celestial religions were only based on the call to discuss accepted ideas and deeply rooted customs in heathen times."

"You then consider discussing accepted ideas as lawful?"

"Yes, and more than that. It is a social necessity. We are now in the process of preparing for the twenty-first century, and therefore we must discuss accepted ideas that no one has discussed. We must examine them freely and carefully to see if the reasons for them still exist, or have disappeared or weakened. They remained as customs and became deeply rooted through petrifaction and barren sanctification, which resembles heathenism. Heathenism worshipped stone while we worship ideas."

"Then you did not intend to harm the society?"

"On the contrary."

"Thank you."

He then addressed the members of the jury. "Would you consider from my client's statements that she is a saboteur or a reformer? I hope that the bleak picture the prosecution wished to draw of my client has been removed from your minds."

The prosecutor rose in turn to question the defendant, beginning by mocking the word "reformer." He asked the defendant, "Do you acknowledge the existence of morality?"

She said, "Of course I do."

"How would you then describe whoever deliberately destroys this morality?"

"I don't want to repeat what I have already stated, which is that we must first determine the meaning of words, especially big words. For major mistakes happen when we use and accept a big word before we examine it. What is meant by the word 'morality'?"

"It is what society regards as its morals."

"We must also specify that society as a particular one at a particular time. Morals of past times and past societies considered a woman who smoked as being immoral, and the one who did not wear a hat was considered uninhibited. Formal evening wear for men was a tuxedo and a white starched shirt that choked them all night, while women's formal wear was an off-the-shoulder bare-backed gown, and whoever went to a formal party dressed otherwise would be considered as violating propriety, etiquette, and good behavior."

At this point, there arose loud laughter from those present and the judge had to bang with his gavel to restore order. The prosecutor looked annoyed, as he saw the defendant's answer heading in a direction he did not want. He said to her, "You know that we are talking about our contemporary society and you are transgressing the laws of this society. Do you admit to that?"

"Please specify to me these laws which I am said to have transgressed."

"Firstly your intent to sabotage the Statue of Liberty."

"If the jury and the court are convinced that I'm guilty and my intention was really sabotage then I am prepared for the penalty."

"Secondly, your admission that you went to the priest to perform an illegal marriage with your partner."

"Where is the crime in that? We didn't do anything in secret. We didn't forge a certificate. And we didn't use any pressure or act of terrorism. We went in broad daylight, very sweetly and politely asked the priest to wed us. He refused and explained that this was unacceptable, and so we left. This matter ended as far as we were concerned, and we believed that the priest on his part would inform the concerned authorities, and that the uproar which we desired would break out."

"Then you've just admitted in court that your intention is to draw attention to the fact that you want to demolish the moral values that the society believes in."

"What's wrong with attracting attention? Isn't that our right?"

"Is it your right to spread the idea of demolishing moral values?"

"Isn't it our right to examine and analyze the truth of such morals?"

"Who gave you this right?"

"The brain in our heads that thinks."

"If everyone gives himself the right to breach the existing system, everything will be destroyed!"

"Sometimes there is no destruction in that but, rather, reform."

"How is that?"

"Something similar happened one day when Jesus Christ entered the temple and ejected the merchants. They considered this at the time a breach of the existing system of that era."

"Was Christ an ordinary person?"

"From his society's point of view, he was. The people and authorities . . . most of them considered him an ordinary person."

"And what was the outcome? Didn't they arrest him and send him to trial to be crucified like anybody else?"

"After he finished his mission."

"What was his mission?"

"Love and peace among mankind."

"Do you believe in Christ?"

"Of course, because I believe in love and peace."

"And do you believe in the teachings of the Church and the laws of Christianity?"

"Whoever believes in love and peace believes in everything."

"Don't evade the answer. I want a definite answer. Do you believe in the prevailing moral values in the society in accordance with the teachings of the Church?"

"Don't frighten us always with the words 'moral values.' We only know one value, which is not causing harm to anyone and excelling in work that is of benefit to others."

"Like thinking of setting fire to the Library of Congress?"

At this point, the lawyer for the defendant strongly objected. He rebuked the prosecutor for his continual allusions to a thought that had come to the mind of his client that she had not taken seriously. He asked him to review the documents in the case files including the certificates of excellence and merit from her university and certificates of recommendation and appraisal from her employers at the Library of Congress. The prosecutor listened for a while, then raised his head and continued the questioning. "There is no objection to your academic and professional excellence. But the accusation is directed at your social deviance."

"When the society itself is deviant, everything else seems to be so!"

"Why can't you be the deviant one and thus regard the society as such?"

"This society has to prove, therefore, that it has not deviated towards aggression and that it is not an aggressive society that is dangerous to world peace."

"If you think you have the right to heap accusations on this society, and to work with other deviant and reckless young people to sabotage its foundations and destroy its values, isn't it a necessary duty for this society to pursue you with all means at its disposal, to reprimand and punish you and bring you back to the right path?"

"The right path? What right path? No one can trust a 'right path' that comes from a society that has destroyed our trust in it and made the horizons of our future red with blood. The crisis of the age is that we have lost trust."

"Don't you see that you are victims of excessive pampering by your society and the only way to reform you is by treating you harshly?"

"And we are waiting hopefully for this harshness?"

"Hopefully? What does that mean?"

"It means that any resistance against us on your part will not succeed, and it will lead to increasing the revolt against you, then to an explosion."

"Do you think that suppression and punishment will be useless?"

"Try. Crucify us as Christ was crucified. They raised him on that piece of timber and the whole of mankind saw him and will go on seeing him and hearing his voice saying, 'Father forgive them, for they know not what they do.' We too will say, 'Forgive the people of our age, for they do not know in what society they live.'"

"Don't you like anything at all in this society? Do you want to cast stones at everything in it?"

"No, not at all. There are great and beautiful things that must be preserved and passed on to the new generations, the new age and the twenty-first century."

"And who should preserve and pass them on? These new generations of young people who are lost, drugged, careless, destructive, destitute, who wander about aimlessly and sleep in the streets?"

"Those, as we have said, are the sacrificial vanguard, the suicide squads, the migratory birds that fall into the sea so that the rest may reach land safely. They lead all the revolutions of history by raising the banners of defiance and shouting the first loud and confused cries using extremist slogans. Their bold ideas intermingle with thoughtless and tumultuous riots. But after this comes the revolution."

"What do you mean here by the revolution?"

"I mean the real revolution of young people, which began like all revolutions with some aspects and the refusal of guardianship over their new lifestyle. They want to feel that something has changed in their lives and to begin bearing their huge responsibilities to change the face of the world."

"And how can they change the face of the world? By disfiguring its features?"

"Yes, its bad and ugly features. You must remember that these new generations, whom you see outwardly having fun, are after all those who fill the seats in universities and libraries, wholeheartedly engaged in carrying out research in labs using the microscope. They will be the ones to make an inventory of and analyze all the great and useful achievements of humanity, to add to them and transfer them to the twenty-first century. All they require from you is to slightly reduce the lecturing and reprimanding directed at them and the urge to oppress and suppress, for the new generation have the instinct for civilized survival. They know their duty to preserve human civilization and to continue with it on the path of development and progress in their own new lifestyle not with your lifestyle!"

"You did not answer the accusation but tried to evade an answer with rhetoric. In brief, do you admit planning to sabotage the Statue of Liberty? Answer yes or no!"

"No!"

"That is sufficient. Thank you."

He turned to the jury and said, "As you have noticed, the defendant and her accomplices insist on denying tangible facts and covering the crime with a smoke curtain of resonant phrases. They reiterate that the case is the case of the twenty-first century, but the truth is that it is one of sabotage of the capitalist imperial society. Your society, our society that we were raised in. You must bear this in mind."

The judge adjourned the session to the next day.

But the next day, I could not rise from my bed. I fell ill from eating meals in American restaurants that my stomach could not accept. As soon as I saw my friend the journalist, I expressed my wish to return to my homeland on the first plane. He tried to convince me to wait until we knew the verdict in the case. I told him the verdict did not interest me; it was the case itself that mattered to me and through it I had discovered many things. So he complied. He reserved a seat for me on the plane and bade me a warm farewell. Soon I was flying above the Statue of Liberty and recollecting what was said about it. I arrived home safely. As soon as I regained some of my health, I picked up a pen and began to write down in these lines what I had seen and heard.

Index

For names beginning with al-, see latter part of name.